Hear Our Prayer
An anthology for collective worship
Kevin Mayhew

Kevin Mayhew

First published in 1996 by
KEVIN MAYHEW LTD
Rattlesden
Bury St Edmunds
Suffolk IP30 0SZ

© 1996 Kevin Mayhew Ltd

The right of Kevin Mayhew to be identified as the author
of this work has been asserted by him in accordance with
the Copyright, Designs and Patents Act 1988.

All rights reserved. No part of this publication may be
reproduced, stored in a retrieval system, or transmitted,
in any form or by any means, electronic, mechanical,
photocopying, recording or otherwise,
without the prior written permission
of the publisher.

The prayers in this book have been extracted and adapted
from *To Speak in Your Presence* by Kevin Mayhew,
published in 1995 by Kevin Mayhew Ltd.

ISBN 0 86209 756 8
Catalogue No 1500039

Front cover: *The Holy Family* by Gandolfi
Reproduced by kind permission of the Rafael Valls Gallery, London.
Cover design by Veronica Ward and Graham Johnstone

Typesetting and Page Creation by Vicky Brown
Printed and bound in Great Britain.

Foreword

I hope that this book will be a welcome and valuable resource for those who have the responsibility of leading prayer in public worship. It contains a rich mixture of prayers from many ages and traditions – prayers from the past, whose fine language and spiritual depth have earned them an honoured place in the devotional life of the church over the centuries, alongside modern prayers which express with beauty, clarity and feeling the aspirations of Christians today.

In our private prayers we need not always use words which are polished or even articulate (though this can, of course, be helpful). St Paul wrote, 'We do not even know how we ought to pray, but through our inarticulate groans the Spirit himself is pleading for us, and God who searches our inmost being knows what the Spirit means' (Romans, chapter 8, verses 26 and 27. R.E.B).

However, in public prayer 'inarticulate groans' will not do, because although God understands what we mean, it is important the congregation do also. Otherwise they will have no part in the conversation. In public prayer, the words used are crucial, not only to hold the congregation's attention but to be a fitting expression of the prayer of the whole church together. The leader of corporate prayer does not pray on the people's behalf, but offers them the means by which they can *all* join in prayer as one body – the body of Christ.

Indeed, the entire act of worship, from hymns to communion and from readings to sermon, is an opportunity and invitation to prayer. But the spoken prayers have a special role in making explicit the church's reaching out to God in faith and becoming open to his grace. Therefore, good prayers, like good poems, should be capable of articulating the thoughts, emotions and concerns of the worshippers, stimulating their imagination, and making them more aware of God and his love for the world.

The church, in more than one sense, stands between the world and God. In its sinfulness, blindness and weakness it becomes a stumbling block which gets in the way of the world's salvation, but by its honest prayer it opens up a channel by which God's Spirit can break through to humankind. It is as if that thread by which the world seems too often to be hanging is the thread of prayer which links it to God's will and purpose.

Traditionally, prayers have been categorized under such headings as Adoration, Thanksgiving, Confession, Intercession, Petition and Dedication. All these themes have been covered within the slightly broader terms of the contents of this book which, together with the indices, should prove helpful in the selection of prayers appropriate to particular times and occasions.

KEVIN MAYHEW

Contents

Prayers of Invocation	7
Prayers for Grace	15
Prayers of Love and Peace	29
Prayers of Joy, Praise and Thanksgiving	35
Prayers of Repentance and Forgiveness	43
Prayers of Faith and Commitment	53
Prayers in Time of Trouble	69
Prayers for the World, Church and People	77
Prayers for Morning and Evening	99
Prayers of Blessing and Commendation	111
Indices	117
Acknowledgements	125

Prayers of Invocation

PRAYERS OF INVOCATION

Come, Holy Spirit, fill our hearts 1
    and enkindle within them the fire of your love.
Send forth your Spirit
    to re-create our hearts and renew your creation.
As you have taught all your people by the light of the Holy Spirit,
    grant that by the gift of the same Spirit we may find wisdom
    and always rejoice in his consolation.

Author unknown

O Christ, deep water of joy, 2
    We long to drink from you!
Come, Lord, in your eager love:
    free us from our sinfulness;
    fill us with your praise;
    and we will sing your glory.

Carmelite Monastery, Quidenham

Holy Spirit, Lord and giver of life, be present. 3
  In our weakness, be our strength;
  in our tiredness, be our freshness;
  in our dirtiness, be our cleansing;
  in our blindness, be our vision;
  in our coldness, be our fervour;
  in our meanness, be our generosity;
  in our hard-heartedness, be our gentle compassion;
  in our stupidity, be our clarity;
  in our arrogance, be our humility;
  in our complexity, be our simplicity;
  in our anxiety, be our peace;
  in our hurt, be our healing;
  in our suffering, be our consolation;
  in our troubles, be our calm;
  in our doubts and despondency, be our hope;
  in our sin, be our forgiveness, mercy and salvation;
for the sake of Jesus and the glory of the Father.

Alan Rees OSB (b. 1941)

[handwritten annotation: In our darkness – be our light.]

4   Soul of Christ, sanctify us.
    Body of Christ, fill us.
    Blood of Christ, save us.
    Water from the side of Christ, wash us.
    Passion of Jesus, strengthen us.
    O good Jesus, hear us.
    Let us not be separated from you.
    From the malicious enemy defend us.
    In the hour of death, call us,
        and bid us come to you,
    that with your saints we may praise you
        for ever and ever.

Pope John XXII (1249-1334)

5   You possess us, Lord,
        and we possess you.
    You have put your faith and hope in us,
        and we have put our faith and hope in you.
    Our lives, our honour,
        our happiness, our peace,
        all rest on you.
    You can see every second of our lives;
        let us see you.
    We pray that you will grant us a single moment
        when we can look at you face to face.
    Then we will be able to give you all our hearts,
        all our love.
    Do not wait until we have died,
        but let us see you even here on earth.
    We know that we have no right to ask this favour
        because our hearts are so lukewarm,
        so indifferent.
    Make us worthy of such a privilege;
        make our hearts ready to receive you,
        and our souls ready to see you.

Simeon the Theodidact (c. 949-1022)

6   Shine into our hearts, O Christ,
        with the pure light of your clear knowledge of God,
        and open the eyes of our minds to your teaching,
        for you are the light of our souls and of our whole selves,
        O Christ our friend and our God.

Martin Shaw

PRAYERS OF INVOCATION

With all our hearts, O Lord,   7
we long for you:
fulfil our loving, longing hope.
Take us in your arms
   and keep us safe.

Carmelite Monastery, Quidenham

Lord, this is your feast,   8
   prepared by your longing,
   spread at your command,
   attended at your invitation,
   blessed by your own word,
   offered by your own hand,
   the undying memorial of your sacrifice upon the cross,
   the full gift of your everlasting love,
   and its perpetuation until time shall end.
Lord, this is bread of heaven, bread of life:
   whoever eats it will hunger no more.
And this is the cup of pardon, healing, gladness, strength:
   whoever drinks it will never thirst again.
So may we come, O Lord, to your table;
   Lord Jesus, come to us.

Eric Milner-White (1884-1964)

Help us, Lord,   9
   always to wait for you,
   to wish for you
   and to watch for you,
   so that at your coming you may find us ready.
For your sake we ask it.

Author unknown

Show us your face,   10
   O Lord, unseen King,
   that our joy may be complete.
Living with you
   we shall become like you.

Carmelite Monastery, Quidenham

11 Eternal Light, shine into our hearts,
Eternal Goodness, deliver us from evil,
Eternal Power, be our support,
Eternal Wisdom, scatter the darkness of our ignorance,
Eternal Pity, have mercy upon us,
 that with all our heart and mind
 and soul and strength
 we may seek your face
 and be brought by your infinite mercy
 to your holy presence,
 through Jesus Christ our Lord.

Alcuin of York (c. 735-804)

12 Spirit of God,
 powerful and unpredictable as the wind,
 you came upon the followers of Jesus at Pentecost
 and swept them off their feet,
 so that they found themselves doing
 what they thought they never had it in them to do.
 It is you who, through all ages,
 have fired people with enthusiasm
 to go about telling the good news of Jesus
 and serving other people for his sake.
Spirit of God,
 powerful and unpredictable as the wind,
 come upon us as we worship
 and become the driving force of our lives.

From Contemporary Prayers

13 O heavenly King, Comforter, Spirit of truth,
 you are found in every place and fill all things,
 source of abundant blessings and giver of life.
Come and live in us,
 cleanse us from all impurity,
 and by your goodness fit us for eternal life.

Eastern Orthodox

Stay with us, Lord Jesus, 14
    so that we shall begin to shine as you shine,
    as a light to others.
The light will be all from you.
It will be you who shine through us upon others.
Give light to them as well as to us;
    light them with us, through us.
Help us witness to you without preaching;
    not by words but by example
    and by the sympathetic influence of what we do;
    by our visible resemblance to your saints
    and the evident fullness of our love for you.

John Henry Newman (1801-1890)

Lord, you humble yourself. 15
You bow down like a servant.
You give yourself always for us.
Teach us to learn from you
    how to love,
    how to hold nothing back,
    how to give ourselves.
Fill us with your Spirit,
    that Spirit of loving and serving
    all our brothers and sisters sincerely,
    without counting the cost.

Liturgical Institute, Trier

Lord, put your hands on our eyes, 16
    that we shall be able to see not only
    that which is visible
    but also that which is invisible.
Let our eyes be focused not only on
    that which is present
    but also on that which is to come.
Unseal our heart's visions,
    that we may gaze on you in your glory.

Origen (c. 185-254)

17   We pray, Lord, that everything we do
       may be prompted by your inspiration,
       so that every prayer and work of ours
       may begin from you
       and be brought by you to completion.

Based on the Prologue of St Benedict's Rule

18   Lord Jesus Christ, pierce our souls with your love
       so that we may always long for you alone,
       who are the bread of angels
       and the fulfilment of the soul's deepest desires.
    May our hearts always hunger and feed upon you,
       so that our souls may be filled with the
       sweetness of your presence.
    May our souls thirst for you,
       who are the source of life,
       wisdom, knowledge, light
       and all the riches of God our Father.
    May we always seek and find you,
       think upon you,
       speak to you
       and do all things for the honour
       and glory of your holy name.
    Be always our only hope,
       our peace, our refuge and our help
       in whom our hearts are rooted
       so that we may never be separated from you.

St Bonaventure (1221-1274)

*Prayers
for Grace*

Grant, O Lord,   19
> that we may not set our hearts on earthly things,
> but love the things of heaven.

And help us now,
> while we are placed among things that are passing away,
> to cling to those that will last for ever,
> through Jesus Christ our Lord.

Leonine Sacramentary (5th Century)

Almighty and ever-living God,   20
we approach the sacrament of your only-begotten Son,
> the Lord Jesus Christ.

We come sick to the doctor of life,
> unclean to the fountain of mercy,
> sightless to the radiance of eternal light,
> poor and needy to the Lord of heaven and earth.

Lord, in your great generosity,
> heal our sickness,
> wash away our defilement,
> enlighten our blindness,
> enrich our poverty,
> and clothe our nakedness.

May we receive the bread of angels,
> the King of kings and Lord of lords,
> with humble reverence,
> with purity and faith,
> with the repentance and love
> and with the determined purpose
> that will help to bring us to salvation.

May we receive the sacrament of the Lord's body and blood,
> and its reality and power.

Kind God,
> may we receive the body of your only begotten Son,
> the Lord Jesus Christ,
> born from the womb of the virgin Mary,
> and so be received into his mystical body
> and numbered among the members of his church.

Loving Father,
> as on our earthly pilgrimage
> we now receive your beloved Son
> under the veil of a sacrament,
> may we one day see him face to face in glory,
> who lives and reigns with you for ever.

St Thomas Aquinas (c.1225-1274)

21   Take away from us, O God,
        all pride and vanity,
        all boasting and forwardness,
    and give us the true courage
        that shows itself by gentleness;
    the true wisdom
        that shows itself by simplicity;
    and the true power
        that shows itself by modesty.

Charles Kingsley (1819-1875)

22   O God our Father, direct and control us in every part of our lives:
        our tongues, that we speak no false words;
        our actions, that we may do nothing to shame ourselves
    or hurt others;
        our minds, that we may think no evil or bitter thoughts;
        our hearts, that they may be set only on pleasing you.

Catholic Prayer Book

23   Guard our eyes, O Lord,
        so that seeing other people's wealth
        will not make us covetous.
    Guard our ears,
        so that they will not listen to foolish
        and malicious gossip.
    Guard our hearts,
        so that we shall not take pleasure
        in the temptations of the world.
    Guard our hands,
        so that they will not be used for violence
        or for exploiting others.
    Guard our feet upon the gentle earth,
        so that in the bustle of life
        we shall not forget the value of rest.

Based on a traditional Irish prayer

PRAYERS FOR GRACE

Almighty God,   24
to you all hearts are open and all desires known,
and from you no secrets are hidden:
    cleanse the thoughts of our hearts
    by the inspiration of your Holy Spirit,
    that we may perfectly love you
    and worthily praise your holy name.

Author unknown

Lord, we believe in you: 25
    increase our faith.
We trust in you:
    strengthen our trust.
We love you:
    let us love you more and more.
We are sorry for our sins:
    deepen our repentance.

We worship you
    as our first beginning.
We long for you
    as our last end.
We praise you
    as our constant helper,
and call on you
    as our loving protector.

Author unknown

Gracious and holy Father,   26
    give us wisdom to recognise you,
    intelligence to understand you,
    diligence to seek you,
    patience to wait for you,
    eyes to see you,
    hearts to meditate on you,
    and lives to proclaim you,
    through the power of the Spirit of Jesus Christ our Lord.

St Benedict (c.480-547)

27   God grant us
        the serenity to accept the things we cannot change,
        the courage to change the things we can,
        and wisdom to know the difference.

Author unknown

28   Lord God,
        the light of the minds that know you,
        the life of the souls that love you,
        and the strength of the wills that serve you:
        help us so to know you that we may truly love you,
        and so to love you that we may fully serve you,
        whom to serve is perfect freedom.

St Augustine of Hippo (354-430)

29   Grant us, Lord, to know what we ought to know,
        to love what we ought to love,
        to praise what delights you most,
        to value what is precious in your sight,
        and to hate what is offensive to you.
      Let us not judge according to superficial appearances,
      nor condemn on the basis of what others say;
      but may we have the discernment to understand deeper realities,
      and above all things to seek your will.

Thomas à Kempis (c.1380-1471)

30   Holy Lord, teach us the meaning of real success,
        and let us not become enslaved by the values of the world,
        but value holiness more than wealth.
      May we aspire to what is eternal,
        and in that may we be successful.

J. H. Jowett (1864-1923)

Grant, O Lord, that the hands that have taken holy things 31
  may daily bring forth fruit to your glory.
Grant, O Lord, that the lips which have sung your
    praise within the sanctuary
  may glorify you for ever;
    that the ears which have heard the music of your songs
  may be closed to clamour and dispute;
    that the eyes which have seen your great love
  may also see your blessed hope;
    that the tongues which have sung the Sanctus
  may ever speak the truth.
Grant that the feet which have trod in your holy place
  may always walk in the light,
  and that the souls and bodies which have tasted
  of your body and blood
  may ever be restored in newness of life.

Liturgy of Malabar

O God, make the door of this house 32
  wide enough to receive all who need
  human love and fellowship,
  and a heavenly Father's care,
  and narrow enough to shut out all envy,
  pride and hate.
Make its threshold smooth enough to be no
  stumbling block to children,
  nor to straying feet,
  but rugged enough to turn back the tempter's power.
Make it a gateway to your eternal kingdom.

Thomas Ken (1637-1711)

Bless us, O Lord God, with all heavenly grace, 33
  and make us pure and holy in your sight.
May the riches of your glory abound in us;
  instruct us with the word of truth,
  inform us with the gospel of salvation,
  and enrich us in your love.

Gelasian Sacramentary (6th Century)

34   O our God, we offer you all our thoughts,
        words, actions and sufferings;
    and we pray that you will give us your grace
        that we may not offend you this day,
        but may faithfully serve you
        and do your holy will in all things.

Traditional

35   Give us a sense of humour, Lord,
        and also things to laugh about.
    Give us the grace to take a joke against ourselves
        and see the funny side of the things we do.
    Save us from annoyance,
        bad temper,
        resentment against our friends.
    Help us to laugh even in the face of trouble.
    Fill our minds with the love of Jesus,
        for his name's sake.

A. G. Bullivant

36   Lord, help us to remember that all time belongs to you,
        and that we are responsible to you for our use of it.
    Help us neither to waste time
        nor to be so obsessed with saving it
        that we become the slaves of time
        and lose our sense of proportion and values.
    Lord, teach us to use our time to your glory:
        creatively,
        re-creatively,
        in that rhythm of involvement in the world
        and of withdrawal from the world
        which is your will for us.
    Save us both from running away from the world
        into self-centred religiosity
        and from running away from the inner life
        into compulsive busyness.
    Lord, help us to live each day
        so that at the end of it
        there is nothing we cannot share with you,
        nothing for which we cannot thank you.

Margaret Dewey (b. 1923)

Lord Jesus, our Saviour, 37
    let us now come to you.
Our hearts are cold:
    warm them by your selfless love.
Our hearts are sinful:
    cleanse them by your precious blood.
Our hearts are weak:
    strengthen them by your joyous Spirit
Our hearts are empty:
    fill them with your divine presence.
Lord Jesus, our hearts are yours:
    possess them always and only for yourself.

St Augustine of Hippo (354-430)

Our Father, teach us the spirit of true worship. 38
Save us from unnecessary formality,
    and from becoming enslaved to tradition for its own sake.
Let our approach to you be at once reverent and joyful,
    and our fellowship with one another both holy and satisfying.

J. H. Jowett (1864-1923)

O Lord our God, 39
    teach our hearts this day
    where and how to see you,
    where and how to find you.
You have made and remade us,
    and you have given to us
    all the truly good things we possess,
    and still we do not know you.
We have not yet done that for which we were created.
Teach us to seek you,
    for we cannot seek you unless you teach us,
    or find you unless you show yourself to us.
Let us seek you in our longing,
    let us long for you in our seeking.
Let us find you by loving you,
    let us love you when we find you.

St Anselm (1033-1109)

When the master of ceremonies tasted the water that had been turned into wine, he said: 'You have kept the best wine until now.' (John 2:9-10)

40   We do not ask to be filled with wine, Lord.
Ordinary water will be enough;
> though we long sometimes for a more visible discipleship,
> a more obvious way of serving you.

And yet,
> being filled with this plain water, Lord,
> we only ask that you pass
> your hand over it,
> changing its contents,
> with all their inadequacy,
> into your wine.

Graham Jeffery (b. 1935)

41   This is our prayer to you, O Lord:
> Give us the strength to bear our joys and sorrows lightly;
> give us the strength to make our love fruitful in service;
> give us the strength never to disown the poor
> or bow before the abuse of power;
> give us the strength to raise our minds high above petty things,
> and give us the strength lovingly
> to surrender our strength to your will.

Rabindranath Tagore (1862-1941)

42   Father,
> you have given to us so very many gifts.

May we profit by them to grow in your truth,
> for we want to be among those
> who will come into your presence,
> who will share your dwelling place
> at the end of time.

Carmelite Monastery, Quidenham

You, Lord, are the bread of life   43
   and the well of holiness.

Just as you feed us day by day
   with the food that sustains our bodies,
   keeping us alive on earth,
We pray that you will feed our souls
   with the spiritual bread of eternity,
   making us ready for heaven.

Just as you satisfy our bodily thirst
   with cool water from the rivers and streams,
   we pray that you will pour the waters
   of holiness into our souls,
   making our every work and action
   a joyful sign of your love.

St Basil of Caesarea (c.330-379)

Loving God, who sees in humankind   44
nothing that you have not given yourself,
   make our bodies healthy and agile,
   our minds sharp and clear,
   our hearts joyful and contented,
   our souls faithful and loving.
And surround us with the company of people and
   angels who share our devotion to you.
Above all, let us live in your presence,
   for with you all fear is banished
   and there is only harmony and peace.
Let every day combine the beauty of spring,
   the brightness of summer,
   the abundance of autumn
   and the repose of winter.
And at the end of our lives on earth,
   grant that we may see and know you
   in the fullness of your glory.

St Thomas Aquinas (c. 1225-1274)

45 We ask for daily bread, but not for wealth
    lest we forget the poor.
  We ask for strength, but not for power
    lest we despise the meek.
  We ask for wisdom, but not for learning
    lest we despise the simple.
  We ask for good repute, but not for fame
    lest we demean the lowly.
  We ask for peace of mind, but not for idle hours
    lest we fail to respond to the call of duty.

Inazo Nitobe

46 Lord, when we think only of our own wants and desires,
  we are impatient to have them satisfied;
    yet in our hearts we know that such satisfaction
    will crumble to dust.
  Give us that spirit of hope which can
    enable us to want what you want,
    and to wait patiently on your time
    in the knowledge that in you alone
    is found true and lasting pleasure.

Mozarabic Sacramentary (3rd century)

47 Holy God, you have shown us light and life.
  You are stronger than any natural power.
  Accept the words from our hearts
    that struggle to reach you.
  Accept the silent thoughts and feelings
    that are offered to you.
  Clear our minds of the clutter of useless facts.
  Bend down to us, and lift us up in your arms.
  Make us holy as you are holy.
  Give us a voice to sing of your love to others.

From a papyrus (probably 2nd-4th century)

How good you are, Lord,   48
and how near to us
– so near that we may always talk to you,
    be comforted by you,
    breathe through you,
    be enlightened by you,
    find peace in you,
    and gain spiritual nourishment from you.
Grant that our fellowship with you
    may never be polluted by malice,
    pride, envy, greed,
    gluttony or falsehood.
Grant that we may belong wholly to you.

John Sergieff (1829-1908)

Prayers of Love & Peace

O God, generous giver to your children,   49
    keep us from envy toward our friends and neighbours,
    and from every form of jealousy.
Teach us to rejoice in what others have which we have not,
    to delight in what they achieve which we cannot accomplish,
    to be glad in all that they enjoy which we do not share;
and so fill us daily more and more with love.

William Angus Knight (1836-1916)

Almighty and most merciful God,   50
    you have given a new commandment
    that we should love one another.
Give us grace to fulfil it.
Make us gentle, courteous and tolerant.
Direct our lives so that we may look to the good of others
    in word and deed.
Sanctify all our friendships by the blessing of your Spirit,
    for the sake of your Son Jesus Christ.

Brooke Foss Westcott (1825-1901)

At the still centre of our being,   51
    let us hear your voice.
    Let it carry us through to the kingdom of heaven
    that exists and breathes within us.
At the still centre of our being,
    let us hear your voice that has existed in all time,
    calling us to the union of peace and love.
At the still centre of our being,
    let the hope born with us break forth in joy.
At the still centre of our being,
    let the seeds sown in love,
    nourished in love,
    grow into bright and glorious flowers,
    rich in fruit.
At the still centre of our being,
    let us rest in love.

Jenny Hunt

52 God of love, through your only Son
        you have given us a new commandment
        that we should love one another as you loved us,
        the unworthy and wandering.
    Give to us, throughout our lives on earth,
        minds ready to forget past ill will,
        pure consciences
        and hearts to love others.

Coptic Liturgy of St Cyril (5th Century)

53 Bless our homes, Father,
        that we cherish the bread
            before there is none,
    discover each other
            before we leave,
    and enjoy each other
            for what we are
            while we have time.

Author unknown

54 Lord God, the source of all holy desire,
    good plans and right actions:
        give us your peace,
        which the world cannot give,
        so that, free from the fear of our enemies,
        we may obey your commandments
        and live in rest and quietness.
    We ask this through the merits of Jesus Christ our Saviour.

Gelasian Sacramentary (6th Century)

55 Father God,
        scripture teaches that to obey Jesus
        is to live within his love,
        just as he, in obeying you,
        lived within yours.
    Help us truly to learn this,
        so that we may be filled with joy;
        let our cup of joy overflow.

Based on John 15:9-11

PRAYERS OF LOVE AND PEACE

O God, let us be united:
   let us speak in harmony;
   let our minds share understanding.
May we be one in our prayer,
   one in the purpose of our meeting,
   one in our resolution,
   one in all our deliberations.
Let our feelings be alike,
   our hearts be unified,
   our intentions the same.
Let our unity be perfect.

Based on the Hindu Scriptures

56

Lord Jesus, in you the perfect love of God is shown:
   hold us firm in this vision,
   always open to your call.
You heal all creation by the offering of your life:
   transfigure us with love,
   make us holy, make us perfect.
As you gave yourself to heal the world,
   may we give ourselves to you and to others.

Richard Garrard (b. 1937)

57

O Lord,
   we believe, and know, and feel
   that you are the supreme Good.
We believe that all the wonder of your creation
   is of no account compared with you.
And therefore,
   since we recognise you as being so beautiful,
   we love you and long to love you more and more.
O God,
   you know how little we love you;
we should not be able to love you at all,
   except for your grace.
Keep our whole being centred on you.
Let us never lose sight of you,
   and let our love for you grow
   more and more every day.

John Henry Newman (1801-1890)

58

59   Lord, make us willing to be used by you.
May our knowledge of our unworthiness
    never make us resist being used by you.
May the need of others always be remembered by us,
    so that we may ever be willing to be used by you.
And open our eyes and our hearts that we may this coming day
    be able to do some work of peace for you.

Alan Paton (1903-1988)

60   Father, enlarge our sympathies;
    give us roomier hearts.
May our lives be like a great welcoming tree
    in whose shade the wanderer may rest.

Create in us the spirit of gentleness,
    and let us touch the wounds of the world with gentle compassion.
Save us from all unthinking severity
    and from harshness of judgement.

J. H. Jowett (1864-1923)

61   Dear Lord,
    it seems that you are so madly
    in love with your creation
    that you could not live without us.
So you created us;
    and then, when we turned away from you,
    you redeemed us.
You are God.
Your greatness is made no greater by our creation;
    your power is made no stronger by our redemption.
Yet you care for us as your own,
    not out of duty but out of love.
It is love, and love alone,
    which moves you.

Catherine of Sienna (c.1347-1380)

Prayers of Joy, Praise & Thanksgiving

We thank you, Lord, for knowing us　　　　　　　　　　　62
　　better than we know ourselves,
and for letting us know ourselves
　　better than others know us.
Make us, we pray,
　　better than they suppose,
　　and forgive us for what they do not know.

　　　　　　　　　　　　　　Possibly by Abu Bekr (d. 634)

Holy God, may the glories of your creation　　　　　　　63
　　awaken our hearts to beauty and song.
Dispel the wintry coldness of our hearts
　　by the incoming of your Spirit,
　　that we may know your true joy.
Refine our souls by your Spirit,
　　and make us more aware of the things of true worth.
Help us to hear your still small voice.

　　　　　　　　　　　　　　　　J. H. Jowett (1864-1923)

O God, we thank you for this universe;　　　　　　　　64
　　for its vastness and its riches,
　　and for the variety of life which teems within it
　　and of which we are a part.
We praise you for the sky and the winds,
　　for the clouds
　　and for the constellations of the heavens.
We praise you for seas and rivers,
　　for mountains and trees,
　　and the grass beneath our feet.
We thank you for the senses which enable
　　us to see the splendour of the morning,
　　to hear the songs of the birds,
　　and enjoy the scents of springtime.
Open our hearts, we pray,
　　to all this joy and beauty,
　　and save us from being so burdened by care
　　or blinded by greed
　　that we fail to notice when even the thornbushes
　　are aflame with your glory.

　　　　　　　　　　　　　　Walter Rauschenbusch (1861-1918)

65   O Lord our God, we pray to you, the supreme truth,
        for all truth comes from you.
    We bring our prayers to you the highest wisdom:
        the wise are such through you.
    You are the supreme joy:
        all true happiness comes from you.
    You are the highest good:
        from you all love and beauty spring.
    You are the Light of the intellect:
        from you comes all human understanding.

Adapted from King Alfred (849-899)

66   Thanks be to you, our Lord Jesus Christ,
        for all the blessings you have won for us,
        for all the pains and insults you have borne for us.
    O most merciful Redeemer, friend and brother,
        may we know you more clearly,
        love you more dearly,
        follow you more nearly,
        now and for ever.

St Richard of Chichester (1197-1253)

67   O Lord, we praise and glorify you
    for all the benefits we have received;
        we bless you, we thank you,
        our hearts sing of your great goodness,
        and in humble love we acclaim you.
    Glory be to you, our benefactor and saviour.

Eastern Orthodox

68   Lord of all mercy and goodness,
        let us not by any ingratitude
        or hardness of heart
        forget the wonderful benefits
        that you have bestowed upon us
        this and every day;
    but grant that we may be mindful,
        all the days of our lives,
        of the incomparable gifts
        which you always give to us.

Traditional Scottish prayer

Glory to you, O God, creator and Father,   69
    for the universe in which we live,
    and for humanity, made in your own image.
Glory to you, O Christ,
    who took a human body
    and redeemed our fallen nature.
Glory to you, O Holy Spirit,
    whose will it is that we should be made whole
    in body, mind and spirit.
Glory to God to all eternity.

George Appleton (1902-1993)

O God, we know you love us!   70
Our hearts are all joy because of what you have done for us.
How good you have been to us, O God most high;
    in our joy we shall sing and delight.
We shall sing in your honour.

Carmelite Monastery, Quidenham

Praise be to you, O God,   71
    who answer us when we call upon you,
    slow though we are to answer you when you call us.
Praise be to you, O God,
    who give to us when we ask,
    miserly though we are when you ask of us.
Praise be to you, O God,
    to whom we confide our needs and they are satisfied.
Praise be to you, O God,
    for you are most worthy of praise.

Based on a Muslim prayer

Set our hearts on fire with love for you, O Christ our God,   72
that in its flame we may love you with all our hearts,
    with all our minds,
    with all our souls
    and with all our strength,
    and our neighbours as ourselves,
so that keeping your commandments we may glorify you,
the giver of all good gifts.

Kontakion (Eastern Orthodox)

73   Let all homage be given to you, Perfect Wisdom:
        you are boundless, you are above all human thought;
        you are faultless, you are without blemish;
        you are spotless, you are greater than space itself.

   As the moonlight depends on the moon,
      so all wisdom depends on your wisdom.
   As the sunlight depends on the sun,
      so all virtue depends on your virtue.

   Those who are constantly concerned with the welfare of others
      are blessed by you in their efforts.
   You are like a mother to the soul,
      giving birth to love, and nourishing virtue.

   As the stars dance round the moon,
      so righteous souls dance round your throne.
   As white clouds encircle the sun,
      so pure souls encircle your throne.

   As the drops of dew evaporate
      when the hot rays of the sun appear,
      so all evil and falsehood evaporate
      under the warmth of your love and truth.

   There are some who have no affection for you,
      and some who look upon you with hatred.
   You do not condemn or destroy them,
      but they condemn themselves to hopeless misery.

   Never to look upon your brightness,
      never to hear your eternal music,
      never to feel your softness,
      is to live without pleasure or joy.

   Those who are devoted to you
      are slaves to your power.
   Yet in obeying your commands of love,
      the soul finds perfect freedom.

   Those who are cold and indifferent to you
      imagine they enjoy perfect freedom.
   Yet they are slaves to their own desires,
      bound in chains by their bodily warmth.

You are the only path to salvation;
   there is no other way but you.
You are the saviour of the world;
   the world is lost without you.

No words can properly describe you;
   the soul alone can know you.
The silent love of the soul
   is the true chorus of praise.

Rahulabhdra (2nd Century)

74

We thank you, God, for the saints of all ages,
for those who in times of darkness
   kept the lamp of faith burning,
for the great souls who saw visions of larger truths
   and dared to declare them,
for the multitude of quiet, gracious souls
   whose presence purified and sanctified the world;
and for those known and loved by us who have passed
   from this earthly fellowship into the fuller life with you.
Accept this our thanksgiving, through Jesus Christ,
   to whom be praise and dominion for ever.

Fellowship Litanies

75

Almighty God, Lord of heaven and earth,
in whom all creation lives and moves
and has its being:
   you are good to all people,
   making your sun to rise on the evil and on the good,
   and sending rain on the just and the unjust.
Look favourably on me your servant
   as I call upon your name,
and send me your blessings from heaven,
   in giving fruitful seasons
   and meeting my needs with food and gladness;
that both my heart and my mouth
   may be continually filled with your praise,
and I may ever give thanks to you in your holy church.

John Cosin (1595-1672)

76   May you be blessed for ever, Lord,
        for not abandoning us when we abandoned you.
    May you be blessed for ever, Lord,
        for offering your hand of love in our darkest,
        most lonely moments.
    May you be blessed for ever, Lord,
        for putting up with such stubborn souls as ours.
    May you be blessed for ever, Lord,
        for loving us more than we love ourselves.
    May you be blessed for ever, Lord,
        for continuing to pour out your blessings upon us,
        even though we respond so poorly.
    May you be blessed for ever, Lord,
        for drawing out the goodness in all people,
        even including us.
    May you be blessed for ever, Lord,
        for repaying our sin with your love.
    May you be blessed for ever, Lord,
        for being constant and unchanging
        amidst all the changes of the world.
    May you be blessed for ever, Lord,
        for your countless blessings on us
        and on all your creatures.

St Teresa of Avila (1515-1582)

Prayers of Repentance & Forgiveness

Most merciful Father, 77
we confess that we have done little
   to promote your kingdom
   and advance your glory.
Pardon our shortcomings
   and give us greater enthusiasm in serving you.
Make us more ready
   and conscientious by our prayers,
   our giving and our example,
   to spread the knowledge of your truth
   and extend your kingdom;
   and may we do everything to your glory.

William Walsham How (1823-1897)

O Holy Spirit of God, 78
   cleanse our eyes to see as you see;
   cleanse our ears to hear you speaking to us;
   cleanse our lips to speak only your words;
   cleanse our minds to discern clearly what is from you;
   cleanse our hearts and fill them with your love,
   love that will overflow to all your people;
   cleanse our bodies and make them more and more your temple;
to the glory and praise of the Father.

Alan Rees OSB (b. 1941)

O God our Father, 79
   you know how often we fail because we are afraid.
We fear what people will do if we stand for the right;
   we fear what they will say.
We fear that we shall not have the strength to go on,
   even if we begin.
Forgive us for our weakness.
Help us to remember Christ
   and all that he endured for us,
   so that we, like him, may never be afraid of people
   but only of sinning against your love.
We ask it for his name's sake.

A. G. Pite

80 Lord God almighty,
  forgive your church
   its wealth among the poor,
   its fear among the unjust,
   its cowardice among the oppressed;
  forgive us, your children,
   our lack of confidence in you,
   our lack of hope in your reign,
   our lack of faith in your presence,
   our lack of trust in your mercy.
  Restore us to your covenant with your people;
   bring us to true repentance;
   teach us to accept the sacrifice of Christ;
   make us strong with the comfort of your Holy Spirit.
  Break us where we are proud;
   make us where we are weak;
   shame us where we trust ourselves;
   name us where we have lost ourselves.

World Council of Churches

81 We love you, Lord Jesus, above all things;
  we repent with our whole heart of ever having offended you.
 Give us grace not to separate ourselves from you again.
 Grant that we may love you always,
  and then let us serve you as you will.

St Alphonsus Liguori (1696-1787)

82 Deliver, O most merciful God,
  all who have strayed into evil ways.
 Do not remember their wrongdoing
  but set them free from enslavement to evil.
 Bless by the power of your Holy Spirit the efforts of all
  who are seeking to influence them for good;
  and grant that, sharing in your heavenly wisdom,
  they may be strengthened to follow your ways.

Robert Leighton (1611-1684)

*Did I not tell you that if you believe in me
you will see the glory of God? (John 11:40)*

Lord, take away the stone from the entrance to our hearts.   83
Let out the stench of corruption, decay and death
   that has been there so long;
let the new person emerge,
   no longer bound by past sins
   but unbound and made free by your healing love.

'Take off the grave clothes and let him go!'

Alan Rees OSB (b. 1941)

O Lord, remember not only the men and women of good will,   84
   but also those of evil will.
But do not remember all the suffering
   they have inflicted upon us;
remember the fruits we have bought, thanks to this suffering:
   our comradeship, our loyalty, our humility,
   our courage, our generosity,
   the greatness of heart which has grown out of all this;
and when they come to judgment,
   let all the fruits we have borne
   be their forgiveness.

*Found near a child's body in Ravensbruch
Women's Concentration Camp*

Lord Christ, who prayed for those who crucified you   85
and commanded your disciples to pray for their enemies,
   forgive those who hate and maltreat us,
   and turn our lives from all harm and evil
   to love shown in action.
For this we humbly pray,
   that, united with all creation,
   we may glorify you
   who alone have perfect love for all people.

Eastern Orthodox

86 Forgive our sins, O Lord;
> the sins of our present and the sins of our past,
> the sins which we have done to please ourselves,
> and the sins which we have done to please others.
>
>Forgive our casual sins and our deliberate sins,
> and those which we have tried so hard to hide
> that we have hidden them even from ourselves.
>
>Forgive us, O Lord, for all of them,
> for Jesus Christ's sake.

Thomas Wilson (1663-1755)

87 Crucified Jesus,
>we kneel in your presence and contemplate in our minds
> the five wounds of your crucifixion.
>We earnestly pray to be filled
> with the gifts of faith, hope and love,
> with true repentance for our sinfulness
> and a firm intention to change.
>So may the contemplation of your passion be for us
> the means of atonement and salvation.

Based on a traditional prayer

88 Heavenly Father, we confess our sins to you:
> the sins of the past and of the present;
> those hidden and forgotten
> as well as those remembered;
> our sins of thought and desire,
> of word, of deed and of omission;
> the sins that we are too dull of heart to see;
> the sins that others can see and we cannot;
> the sins known to you alone.
>We are sorry for all of them.
>
>We ask you to forgive us
> through the merit of Jesus, our Saviour.
>Please renew your life in us
> by the power of the Holy Spirit.

Alan Rees OSB (b. 1941)

O God, forgive us for all the faults   89
    which make us difficult to live with.

If we behave as if we were the only ones for whom
    life is difficult;
    if we behave as if we were far harder worked than anyone else;
    if we behave as if we were the only ones ever to be
    disappointed or to get a raw deal;
    if we are far too self-centred and far too full of self-pity:
forgive us, O God.

If we are too impatient to finish the work we have begun;
    if we are too impatient to listen to someone
    who wants to talk to us,
    or to give someone a helping hand;
    if we think that other people are fools,
    and make no attempt to conceal our contempt for them:
forgive us, O God.

If we too often rub people up the wrong way;
    if we spoil a good case by trying to ram it
    down someone's throat;
    if we do things that get on people's nerves,
    and go on doing them even when we are asked not to:
forgive us, O God.

Help us to take the selfishness and the ugliness out of life
    and to do better in the days to come.

William Barclay (1907-1978)

Lord, forgive us our sins: 90
    our lack of faith,
    our lack of hope,
    our lack of love.
We look to you,
    kind and gracious God.
Our hearts are open.
Please give us
Faith, Hope and Love.

Alan Rees OSB (b. 1941)

91   Lord, when we think that our hearts are overflowing with love
          and realise in a moment's honesty that it is only
          ourselves that we love in the loved one,
          deliver us from ourselves.

      Lord, when we think we have given all that we have to give
          and realise in a moment's honesty that
          it is we who are the recipients,
          deliver us from ourselves.

      Lord, when we have convinced ourselves that we are poor
          and realise in a moment's honesty that
          we are rich in pride and envy,
          deliver us from ourselves.

      And, Lord, when the kingdom of heaven merges deceptively
          with the kingdoms of this world,
          let nothing satisfy us but you.

Mother Teresa (b. 1910)

92   O Light everlasting, surpassing all created light!
      Pour forth from heaven the glorious rays of your light,
          and pierce the dark depths of our souls.
      Purify, gladden and enlighten our souls,
          that they may turn to you in joy.
      We know that the shadow of sin still hangs over us;
      we know that we fight against your light,
          preferring the gloom of worldly pride
          to the bright sunshine of true humility.
      Yet you, who can make the raging sea calm,
          can bring peace to our souls.
      You, who turn night into day,
          can bring gladness to our miserable souls.
      Act now!
      Banish darkness at this very moment!
      Inspire our souls with your love at the next breath we take!

Thomas à Kempis (c.1380-1471)

Remember, Lord, what you have promised,   93
    giving your servants great hope.
However low we fall,
    to that promise we cling,
for with you, our God, lies forgiveness.

Carmelite Monastery, Quidenham

O Lord and master of our lives,   94
    take from us the spirit of laziness, faint-heartedness,
    lust for power, and love of gossip.
Give us grace to see our own errors and not to judge others,
    for you are blessed from all ages to all ages.

Eastern Orthodox

Lord, in your loving kindness,   95
    give us the fullness of the Holy Spirit
    to establish us in abundant life.
Grant that we may be better people,
    more loving, more attentive
    and more generous to you and to everyone.

Grant us the Spirit of new life and of healing,
    so that we may be whole in body and soul.
Let your Spirit destroy in us
    the roots of sin and fear;
may he take from us all hardness of heart
    and plant within us your law of love
so that we may grow up into graciousness of life
    and find joy therein.

Alan Rees OSB (b. 1941)

96 What shall we say in your presence,
  you who dwell on high?
What shall we declare to you,
  who are in heaven beyond?
For you know things secret
  as well as revealed.
You know the mysteries of the universe
  and the unconscious thoughts of everyone alive.
You search the innermost parts,
  you watch our motives and our passions.
Nothing is concealed from you.
Nothing is hidden from your gaze.

Lord our God, and God of our ancestors,
  have mercy upon us and pardon our sins.
Forgive our wrongdoings and set aside our misdeeds.
Blot out the wrong that we have done,
  for you, O Lord, are good and forgiving,
  and full of love to all who call upon you.
For your own sake, forgive our great failures.
For your own sake, give us life.
In your righteousness bring our souls out of trouble.
The Lord of all creation is with us.
The God of Jacob is our refuge.
Lord of creation,
  happy are those who trust in you.

Reform Synagogues of Great Britain

Prayers of Faith & Commitment

O God, you have created us
    to do you some definite service;
you have given some definite work to us
    which you have not given to any other.
We have our place in your plan.
We may never know what it is in this life
    but we shall be told it in the next.
Therefore we will trust you in all things.
If we are sick, our sickness may serve you.
If we are worried, our worry may serve you.
If we are in sorrow, our sorrow may serve you.
Nothing is in vain:
    all things may serve your purpose.
We may lose our friends and find ourselves among strangers;
we may feel forgotten so that our spirits sink;
our future may be hidden from us;
still, you work in all things for good,
    and we trust you.

John Henry Newman (1801-1890)

97

Father, make us realise more and more
    that it is only in being stripped of everything
    that we are more given to you;
    and when we are more given to you,
    then are we truly free.
Let us cling to nothing;
    let us lose all to gain all.
Let us never rely on ourselves;
    when we cannot cope
    let us hand everything over to you
    and just trust you,
    remembering that we are your children
    and you care for us.
Let us accept humiliation and the cross with Jesus crucified.
Let us remain hidden and humble in union with your Son.
Let us always remember
    that the only thing that matters
    is to be totally united with your will
    and in this is our peace.
Let our prayer be always Amen! Alleluia!

Alan Rees OSB (b. 1941)

98

99   O Lord, this is our desire:
to walk along the path of life
that you have appointed for us,
    in steadfastness of faith,
    in lowliness of heart,
    in gentleness of love.
Let not the cares or duties of this life
    press upon us too heavily,
    but lighten our burden
    that we may follow your way in quietness,
    filled with thankfulness for your mercy.

Maria Hare (1798-1870)

100   O Lord, give us more love,
    more self-denial,
    more likeness to you.
Teach us to sacrifice our comforts to others,
    to set aside our own preferences
    for the sake of doing good.
Make us kind in thought,
    gentle in word,
    generous in deed.
Teach us that it is better to give than to receive,
    better to forget ourselves than to put ourselves forward,
    better to serve than to be served.
And to you, the God of love,
    be all glory and praise,
    now and for ever.

Henry Alford (1810-1871)

101   O heavenly Father, in whom we live and move
    and have our being,
we humbly pray that you will guide us by your Holy Spirit
    that in all the cares and occupations of our daily lives
    we may never forget you,
    but remember that we are always walking in your sight.

Author unknown

Teach us, good Lord, 102
not to complain about excessive work
  or shortness of time;
not to exaggerate the tasks we undertake
  by pretending to be burdened by them;
  but to accept them all in freedom and joy.
Teach us not to call attention to busyness
  or petty irritations;
not to become so dependent upon others' appreciation of us
  that our motives become suspect;
not to demand respect from other people
  merely on account of our age or past achievements.

Edward Benson (1829-1896)

We ask you, O God, the God of truth, 103
that what we ought to know you will teach us,
that where we are mistaken you will correct us,
that whenever we stumble you will support us,
  and from all that is false,
  all that is damaging,
  you will always protect us.

Brooke Foss Westcott (1825-1901)

O Lord, to whom everything in heaven and earth belongs, 104
we long to commit ourselves wholly to you
  and be yours for ever.
We offer ourselves to you wholeheartedly today
  to serve and obey you
  and offer you constant sacrifice
  of praise and thanksgiving.
Accept us, our Saviour,
  with the offering of your body and blood,
  in the presence of the angels,
  that this sacrifice may be sufficient
  for the redemption of ourselves
  and the whole creation.

Thomas à Kempis (1380-1471)

105 Help us at all times, O God,
> to encourage and not to dishearten,
> to be more ready to praise than to condemn,
> to uplift rather than to disparage,
> to veil rather than to expose the faults of others.

> O risen and exalted Christ, dwell in us,
> that we may live with the light of hope in our eyes,
> the word of life on our lips
> and your love in our hearts.

> Help us, O Holy Spirit,
> to seek you faithfully,
> to hold to you firmly,
> to show you unfailingly,
> for Christ's sake.

T. Glyn Thomas (1905-1973) Tr. W. Rhys Nicholas (b. 1914)

106 All we ask, Lord, is that
> your glory may shine forth in this place.

> All we ask is that
> you give us what is best for us all and for each one.

> All we ask is that
> we may love you and each other personally
> and with our whole heart.

> Help us to surrender all our vain wishes,
> anxieties and desires
> and give all things into your waiting hands.
> Grant us the faith and trust
> that accepts everything from you as a grace,
> a blessing and an opportunity for growth.
> If this causes pain, let us accept it
> and understand it as a transforming experience.
> Help us not to put obstacles in the way of your will,
> nor to give in to sadness and anxiety
> when there is darkness and conflict in our lives.

Alan Rees OSB (b. 1941)

PRAYERS OF FAITH AND COMMITMENT

Lord Jesus,   107
    we give you our hands to do your work;
    we give you our feet to go your way;
    we give you our eyes to see as you do;
    we give you our tongues to speak your words;
    we give you our minds that you may think in us;
    we give you our spirits that you may pray in us.
Above all
    we give you our hearts that you may love in us
    your Father and all humankind.
    We give you our whole selves that you may grow in us,
    so that it is you, Lord Jesus,
    who live and work and pray in us.

The Grail Prayer

Take, Lord, all our liberty.   108
Receive our memories,
    our understanding
    and our whole will.
Whatever we have and possess you have given us;
    to you we restore it wholly
    and to your will we utterly surrender it
    for you to direct us.
Give us love for you only,
    with your grace,
    and we are rich enough;
    nor do we ask for anything else.

St Ignatius Loyola (1491-1556)

Guide us, O Lord,   109
    in all the changes and uncertainties of the world,
    that we remain at peace.
Let us not complain in trouble,
    nor grow proud in prosperity,
    but in calm faith accept your will,
    through Jesus Christ our Lord.

Jeremy Taylor (1613-1667)

HEAR OUR PRAYER

110   Lord, make us so sensitive
        to the needs of those around us
        that we never fail to know
        when they are hurting or afraid;
    or when they are simply crying out
        for someone's touch
        to ease their loneliness.
    Let us love so much
        that our first thought is of others
        and our last thought is of ourselves.

Author unknown

111   Give us courage, O Lord, to stand up and be counted,
        to stand up for those who cannot stand up for themselves,
        to stand up for ourselves when it is appropriate for us to do so.
    Let us fear nothing more than we fear failing you.
    Let us love nothing more than we love you,
        for thus we shall fear nothing indeed.
    Let us have no other God before you,
        whether nation, or party, or state, or church.
    Let us seek no other peace
        but the peace which is yours,
        and make ourselves its instruments,
        opening our minds and our hearts
        so that we shall always know
        what work of peace we may do for you.

Alan Paton (1903-1988)

112   Teach us, good Lord,
        to serve you as you deserve:
        to give, and not to count the cost;
        to fight, and not to heed the wounds;
        to toil, and not to seek for rest;
        to labour, and to ask for no reward,
        except that of knowing that we do your will;
        through Jesus Christ our Lord.

St Ignatius Loyola (1491-1556)

Lord, make us instruments of your peace: 113
    where there is hatred, let us sow love,
    where there is injury, pardon,
    where there is doubt, faith,
    where there is darkness, light,
    where there is despair, hope,
    and where there is sadness, joy.

O divine Master,
grant that we may not so much seek
    to be consoled as to console,
    to be understood as to understand,
    to be loved as to love.
For it is in giving that we receive,
    it is in pardoning that we are pardoned,
    and in dying that we are born to eternal life.

Attributed to St Francis of Assisi (1181-1226)

Lord, make our hearts a haven   114
    where the lonely may find friendship,
    where the weary may find shelter,
    where the helpless may find refuge,
    where the hopeless may find hope,
    where all those who seek someone who cares
    may enter and find you.

Author unknown

Lord, put courage into our hearts,   115
    and take away all that may hinder our serving you.
Free our tongues to proclaim your goodness,
    that all may understand us.
Give us friends to advise and help us,
    that by working together
    our efforts may bear abundant fruit.
And, above all,
    let us constantly remember that our actions are worthless
    unless they are guided by your hand.

Muhammed (570-632)

116 Lord Christ,
   you have no body on earth but ours,
   no hands but ours,
   no feet but ours.
Ours are the eyes through which your compassion
   must look out on the world.
Ours are the feet by which you may still
   go about doing good.
Ours are the hands with which
   you bless people now.
Bless our minds and bodies,
   that we may be a blessing to others.

Based on a prayer by St Teresa of Avila (1515-1582)

117 From the cowardice that dare not face new truth,
   from the laziness that is content with half truth,
   from the arrogance that thinks it knows all truth,
good Lord, deliver us.

Kenyan prayer

118 Lord, make us messengers
      of your love.
   To the searching heart
      send us with your word;
   to the aching heart
      send us with your peace;
   to the broken heart
      send us with your love.
   However small or wide
      our world, Lord,
   let us warm it with the promise
      that you care.

Author unknown

PRAYERS OF FAITH AND COMMITMENT

Lord Jesus, lead us, give us the spirit of prayer.   *119*
Teach us to pray, as you taught your apostles;
    give us courage to go with you
    into the lonely mountains
    and pray to the Father in the secret of our hearts.
Teach us to struggle in prayer
    as you struggled in the garden of Gethsemane.
Draw us closer to yourself and to the Father
    through the Holy Spirit.
Help us to overcome all obstacles,
    and teach us not to be afraid
    when we have to face certain things within ourselves
    which seem to be more than we can cope with.
Help us in naked faith to go on knowing that you are there,
    calling us and drawing us,
    even when all seems dark and arid.
Give us the strength of the Spirit to overcome our fear.
Deepen our friendship with you;
    although we are not worthy of such a gift,
    we know that you want us to have it,
    so we take heart and come to you confidently,
    trusting in the promises you have made.

Alan Rees OSB (b. 1941)

Here we are, Lord – body, heart and soul.   *120*
Grant that, with your love,
we may be big enough to reach the world,
and small enough to be at one with you.

Mother Teresa (b. 1910)

May we do all the good we can,   *121*
    by all the means we can,
    in all the ways we can,
    in all the places we can,
    for all the people we can,
    as long as ever we can,
for Christ's sake.

Based on the Rule of John Wesley (1703-1791)

122   Holy God, give us true faith in you.
In times of doubt and questioning,
   when our belief is confused by new learning,
   new teaching, new thought,
   when our faith is strained by creeds, by doctrines,
   by mysteries beyond our understanding,
give us the faithfulness of disciples
and the courage of believers in you;
give us confidence to examine,
   and faith to trust in, all truth;
stability to hold fast to what is good,
with the benefit of new insights and interpretations;
to acknowledge when fresh truth has been revealed to us,
and in troublesome times genuinely to grasp new knowledge
and to combine it loyally and honestly with the old;
give us the insight to refrain
both from stubborn rejection of new revelations
and from the easy assumption that ours is a more
   enlightened generation.
Save us and help us,
we humbly pray, O Lord.

George Ridding (1828-1904)

123   Most merciful God, order our days
   so that we may know what you want us to do,
   and then help us to do it.
Let us not be elated by success or depressed by failure.
We want only to take pleasure in what pleases you,
   and only to grieve at what displeases you.
For the sake of your love,
   we would willingly forego all temporal comforts.
May all the joys in which you have no part weary us.
Let our thoughts frequently turn to you,
   that we may be obedient to you without complaint,
   patient without grumbling,
   cheerful without self-indulgence,
   contrite without dejection,
   and serious without austerity.
Let us hold you in awe without being terrified of you,
   and let us be an example to others
   without any trace of pride.

St Thomas Aquinas (c. 1225-1274)

Lord, since you exist, we exist; 124
   since you are beautiful, we are beautiful;
   since you are good, we are good.
By our existence we honour you;
   by our beauty we glorify you;
   by our goodness we love you.
Lord, through your power all things were made;
   through your wisdom all things are governed;
   through your grace all things are sustained.
Give us power to serve you,
   wisdom to discern your laws,
   and grace to obey those at all times.

Edmund of Abingdon (c.1180-1240)

Dear Lord, help us keep our eyes on you. 125
You are the incarnation of divine love;
   you are the expression of God's infinite compassion;
   you are the visible manifestation of the Father's holiness.
You are beauty, goodness, gentleness,
   forgiveness and mercy.
Outside you, nothing can be found.
Why should we look elsewhere?
You have the words of eternal life;
   you are food and drink;
   you are the Way, the Truth and the Life.
You are the light that shines in the darkness,
   the lamp on the lampstand,
   the house on the hilltop.
You are the perfection of God.
In and through you we can see and find our way
   to the heavenly Father.
O Holy One, Beautiful One, Glorious One,
   be our Lord and Saviour, our Redeemer,
   our Guide, our Consoler, our Comforter,
   our Hope, our Joy and our Peace.
To you we want to give all that we are.
Let us be generous, not stingy or hesitant.
Let us give you all
   – all we have, think, do and feel.
It is yours, O Lord.
Please accept it, and make it fully your own.

Henri Nouwen (b.1932)

126 Gracious God, we praise and thank you
  that you have preserved us during the past week,
  and blessed the work of our hands.
Through each day
 you have helped us to build
 a temple of prayer in our hearts,
 so that even in the midst of our labours
 we may rejoice in you.
And now on the day of rest
 we may devote all our attention to you.
Let the joy of this day
 be a foretaste of the joy of paradise.
Let this day of worship
 be a sign of the constant and everlasting worship
 around your heavenly throne.

Gracious God,
 help us this day to listen to your teachings,
  that our minds may be refashioned according to your love.
Let us turn deaf ears to all idle and malicious gossip,
 and let us turn blind eyes to all temptation.
Make us new people,
 alert only to your truth,
 and alive only to your grace.
And thus let us celebrate Sunday after Sunday,
 and Sabbath after Sabbath,
 with unstinting devotion,
 until you shall admit us to the unceasing
 celebrations of heaven,
 the eternal Sabbath.

Johann Starck (1680-1756)

127 Lord, inspire us to read your scriptures
  and meditate upon them day and night.
 We beg you to give us real understanding of what we need,
  that we in turn may put its precepts into practice.
 Yet we know that understanding and good intentions
  are worthless unless rooted in your graceful love.
 So we ask that the words of scriptures
  may also be not just signs on a page
  but channels of grace into our hearts.

Origen (c.185-254)

O Lord, do not let us turn into 'broken cisterns' 128
    that can hold no water.
Do not let us be so blinded by the enjoyment
    of the good things of earth
that our hearts become insensitive to the cry of the poor,
    of the sick, of orphaned children
        and of those innumerable brothers and sisters of ours
    who lack the necessary minimum to eat,
    to clothe their nakedness,
    and to gather their families together
    under one roof.

Pope John XXIII (d. 1963)

Dear Lord, we will carry any cross you like, 129
    provided it is not our own.
We find our own weaknesses so hard to bear;
    our own failure;
    our own depression.
And yet, as well as we may, we offer our lives to you.
We ask you to bless them if you can,
    in ways we may never know.
We ask you to use our failure, our breakdown,
    to help others in their quest for faith.
Dear Lord, we offer our lives and our failures to you,
    to be a blessing for others.
Dear Lord, in your way and your time,
    please use us, for Jesus' sake.

Graham Jeffery (b.1935)

Lord, whose way is perfect, 130
help us always to trust in your goodness,
that walking with you
and following you in all simplicity,
we may possess quiet and contented minds
and may cast all care on you,
for you care for us.

Christina Rosetti (1830-1894)

131   O Holy Spirit of God,
           take us as your disciples;
           guide us, enlighten us, sanctify us.
       Control our hands that they may do no evil,
           cover our eyes so that they may see it no more,
           and sanctify our hearts so that evil may not dwell within us.
       Be our God; be our guide.
       Wherever you lead we will go;
           whatever you forbid we will renounce;
           and whatever you command us,
           in your strength we will do.
       Lead us, then, into the fullness of your truth.

Henry E. Manning (1808-1892)

132   Help us, Lord, to let go of whatever keeps our lives
           from being the best they can be:
           the stress, the frustration, the anger,
           the petty jealousies and strong temptations.
       Help us to let go of the need to feel
           that we are in sole charge of our lives.
       Help us to trust you for the strength we need,
           and guide us to that still,
           serene place within ourselves.
       Help us to trust you to show us your way,
           and give us courage and wisdom to follow it.
       May we find renewed peace by committing our lives to you.

Author unknown

133   We surrender ourselves totally to you, Lord.
       We renounce our own will and desires.
       We accept the cross with praise and thanksgiving.
       We will not fight you, Lord,
           nor the difficult people and circumstances
           that come our way.
       We renounce all rebellion
           and place ourselves at the disposal
           of our brothers and sisters
           in trust and serenity.
       We surrender ourselves totally to you, our Lord.

Alan Rees OSB (b. 1941)

Prayers in Time of Trouble

*Peter was sad when Jesus asked him the third time:
'Do you love me?' He replied: 'Lord, you know everything.'*
(John 21:17)

It is not easy repeating oneself, Lord, saying:
   'I love you,
   and I will follow you,'
   for the second and third,
   for the three hundredth time.
Yet we do it,
   as well as we can.
As young men or women first,
   more easily.
Then, when we are older
   and tied down to the world and life
   by a thousand little cords,
   we say again the old words:
   'Lord, you know that I am your friend.'
And though we say it with awkwardness,
   with rheumatism in our limbs
   and tiredness and lost opportunities in our hearts,
   still you hear us,
   and receive us,
   and lead us on.

Graham Jeffery (b. 1935)

Steer the ship of our lives, good Lord,
   to your quiet harbour where we can be safe
   from the storms of sin and conflict.
Show us the course we should take.
Renew in us the gift of discernment,
   so that we can always see the right direction
   in which we should go;
   and give us the strength and the courage
   to choose the right course,
   even when the sea is rough and the waves are high,
   knowing that by suffering hardship
   and danger in your name
   we shall find comfort and peace.

St Basil of Caesarea (c.330-379)

136   Hold our hands, Lord,
        walk us through the loneliness
        and the valley of our sorrows.
    Hold on to us when we're too afraid
        to think about the future.
    Let us lean on you, Lord,
        when we're too weary to continue.
    Hold our hands, Lord, through the night
        until we see the light of dawn.

Author unknown

137   Lord Jesus,
    in your agony in the garden you said,
        'My soul is sorrowful
        to the point of death.'
    We too are now feeling sad and despondent.
    You know the cause.
    The power of your Spirit can give us the remedy.
    Heal us, Lord, of this depression.
    Give us the joy and peace of knowing
        that nothing in our life or death
        can separate us from you.

Author unknown

They made the grave secure; sealed with a stone, and guarded.
(Matthew 27:66)

138   When all hope is gone, Lord,
        you are born.
    When the darkness is complete,
        you come.
    When things are beyond despair,
        we find you.
    You roll back the stone
        and are there to greet us.

Graham Jeffery (b. 1935)

Our Father,   139
    when we are inclined to panic,
    or to act hastily,
    help us to rest in the shadow of your love.
Keep us cool and calm
    in the heat of the world's busyness.
Give us the spirit of humility,
    and keep us from all harshness,
    intolerance and pride.
May we gladly use our strength
    to carry our neighbour's cross.

J. H. Jowett (1864-1923)

Dear Lord,   140
    you see the lives we try to live
    within the lives we live.
Beneath our fears,
    failures and inadequacies,
    you reach down and touch us.
You love us.
You are our friend.

Graham Jeffery (b.1935)

O eternal God,   141
    helper of the helpless,
    comforter of the comfortless,
    hope of the afflicted,
    bread of the hungry,
    drink of the thirsty,
    and saviour of all who wait upon you:
we bless and glorify your name;
we adore your goodness and delight in your love.
Take from us every tendency toward sin or vanity;
    let our desires soar upwards to your love,
    that we may hunger and thirst for the bread of life
    and the wine of heaven,
    and know no love but yours.

Jeremy Taylor (1613-1667)

142   O God of peace,
        unite the hearts of all people
        that we may live with one another
        in gentleness and humility, in peace and unity.
    O God of patience,
        give us patience in times of trouble,
        and courage to endure to the end.
    O Spirit of prayer,
        awaken our hearts
        that we may lift up holy hands to God
        and cry to him in all our distress.
    Be our defence in time of need,
        our help in trouble,
        our consolation when all things seem to be against us.
    Come, eternal light, salvation and comfort;
        be our light in darkness,
        our salvation in life,
        our comfort in death,
        and lead us in the narrow way to everlasting life,
        that we may praise you for ever,
        through Jesus Christ our Lord.

Bernard Albrecht (d.1636)

143   Give us your light, O Lord,
        that the darkness of our hearts may vanish away,
        and we may come to the true light,
        who is Jesus Christ our Lord.

Author unknown

144   Lord, look upon us with the eyes of your mercy.
    May your healing hand rest upon us;
        may your life-giving power
        flow into every cell of our bodies
        and into the depths of our souls,
        cleansing, purifying,
        restoring us to wholeness and strength
        for service in your kingdom.

Author unknown

Lord, hear our voices when we cry to you! 145
Our hearts say:
   we have longed,
   earnestly have we longed,
   to gaze upon your face.
Do not turn your face away from us.
Look tenderly upon your servants
   and, in your love,
   teach us to be free.

Carmelite Monastery, Quidenham

Each day has troubles enough of its own. (Matthew 6:34)

Lord, we ask your blessing 146
   on this moment only.
Nothing else.
The past is the past,
   though we often regret it.
Tomorrow will come,
   and we're often afraid of it.
But this moment only
   can we influence in any way.
And we need your help
   to do it.

Graham Jeffery (b. 1935)

O God, the only source of health and healing, 147
the spirit of calm and the central peace of this universe,
grant us such a consciousness of your indwelling
and surrounding presence that we may accept the health,
strength and peace you are longing to give.

Author unknown

Prayers for the World, Church & People

We bring before you, O Lord,   *148*
    the troubles and perils of people and nations,
    the pain of prisoners and captives,
    the sorrows of the bereaved,
    the needs of strangers,
    the vulnerability of the weak,
    the downheartedness of the weary,
    the diminishing powers of the aged.
O Lord, draw near to each,
    for the sake of Jesus Christ our Lord.

St Anselm (1033-1109)

O God,   *149*
    the creative touch of beauty
    and the wellspring of love,
    blend in our lives the mysterious strength
    that radiates from you the Creator,
    the compassion of you the Son
    and the inspiration of you the Spirit.
May we invigorate the steps of the sad,
    lighten those gripped by darkness,
    and love the unloved and the hearts of stone,
    knowing always the assurance of the stillness
    and the strength of the love
    in Jesus Christ ever present.

Martin Shaw

Grant, O Lord,   *150*
    that none may love you less this day
    because of us;
    that no word or act of ours
    may turn one soul from you;
    and for one more grace we dare to pray,
    that many people may love you more this day
    because of us.

Eric Milner-White (1884-1964)

HEAR OUR PRAYER

151   Almighty and most merciful Father,
       who has taught us not to think only of ourselves
       but also of the needs of others,
we remember before you
       all who are burdened and oppressed,
       those whose hopes have been crushed
       and whose plans have come to nothing.

We remember also
       those who are afflicted by poverty,
       or worn down by sickness and disease,
       those who are in darkness or despair,
       or who are suffering for righteousness' sake.

Help them all, O God,
       to rest in you for comfort and strength.

William Angus Knight (1836-1916)

152   Dear Lord, are we ready to say it yet?
Not 'We believe in one God',
       which is easily said,
       the words tripping,
       appropriately, off our lips.
But your love asks us to go further.
Your love impels us to say:
       'We believe in one world.'

Graham Jeffery (b.1935)

153   Grant us grace, O Father,
       not to pass by suffering or joy without eyes to see.
       Give us understanding and sympathy,
       and guard us from selfishness,
       that we may enter into the joys and sufferings of others.
       Use us to gladden and strengthen those
           who are weak or suffering;
       that by our lives we may help others to believe and serve you,
       and shed forth your light which is the light of life.

Dick Sheppard (1880-1937)

PRAYERS FOR THE WORLD, CHURCH AND PEOPLE

Loving Father,   154
   you have made all people in your likeness,
   and love all whom you have made.
Let not the world separate itself from you
   by building barriers of race and colour.
As your son was born of a Hebrew mother,
   yet rejoiced in the faith of a Syrian woman
   and a Roman soldier,
   welcomed the Greeks who sought after him
   and allowed a man from Africa to carry his cross,
   so teach all people to regard the members of all races
   as fellow heirs of your kingdom,
   through the same, Jesus Christ our Lord.

Toc H Prayer

Lord God, almighty Creator,   155
teach us and all people to understand more and
   more profoundly that every human life is sacred,
whether it belongs to an unborn infant
or to a terminally-ill patient,
to a handicapped child
or to a disabled adult.

Remind us, heavenly Father,
that each individual has been made in your image and likeness
and has been redeemed by Christ.

Help us to see each other with your eyes,
so that we may reverence,
   preserve and sustain your gift of life in them
and use our own lives more faithfully in your service.

Basil Hume (b. 1923)

O Lord and heavenly Father,   156
we commend to your care the people of this land
who are suffering distress and anxiety through lack of work.
Strengthen and support them, we pray;
and so increase the wisdom of those who direct our industries
that people may be set free from want and fear,
to work in peace and security for the relief of their necessities
and the well-being of the nation.

Industrial Christian Fellowship

157   Lord, shake away our indifference and insensitivity to the
        plight of the poor.
When we meet you hungry, thirsty or as a stranger,
show us how we can give you food,
    quench your thirst
    or receive you in our homes
    – and in our hearts.
Show us how we can serve you in the least of your brothers
    and sisters.

Mother Teresa (b. 1910)

158   Save your church, O Lord, from the fear of the truth,
that it may not be found to work against you
    under the cloak of enthusiasm.

Make it ready to follow you along new paths
    when called to do so;
and grant that its knowledge of you be so strong and living
    that it cannot help but sing to you a new song.

In all difficulties and troubles,
intensify in it that love which
    hopes all things,
    endures all things,
    and which never behaves inappropriately,
    but is always willing to be helpful.

Herbert Morgan (1875-1946)

159   Lord Jesus Christ, you are the way of peace.
Come into the brokenness of this world
    with your healing love.
Help us to be willing to bow before you in true repentance,
    and to bow to one another in real forgiveness.
By the fire of the Holy Spirit melt our hard hearts
    and consume the pride and prejudice
    which separate us from each other.
Fill us, O Lord, with your perfect love which casts out fear,
    and bind us together in that unity which you share
    with the Father and the Holy Spirit for ever.

Cecil Kerr

PRAYERS FOR THE WORLD, CHURCH AND PEOPLE

O Lord, grant that we may not be conformed to the world 160
    but may love it and serve it.
Grant that we may never shrink from being
    the instruments of your peace
    because of the judgement of the world.
Grant that we may love you without fear of the world.
Grant that we may never believe that the inexpressible
    majesty of yourself
    may be found in any power of this earth.
May we firstly love you and our neighbour as ourselves.
May we remember the poor and the prisoner,
    the sick and the lonely,
    the young searchers,
    and those without homes,
    the lost and the fearful,
    as we remember Christ who is in them all.
And may we, this coming day,
    be able to do some work of peace for you.

Alan Paton (1903-1988)

God of compassion, 161
    we acknowledge that you travel with those
    who have no resting place.
In your Son's flight into Egypt
    and in his helplessness,
    you took to yourself the heart of the refugee.
Love the forgotten ones who now long for a home but,
    through national and political upheaval, have none;
in Jesus Christ,
the lover of the lost ones,
our light and your love among us.

Martin Shaw

Make us worthy, Lord, 162
    to serve our fellow people throughout the world
    who die in poverty and hunger.
Give them through our hands this day their daily bread,
    and by our understanding love,
    give peace and joy.

Mother Teresa (b.1910)

163   Lord Jesus, when you were on earth,
       they brought the sick to you
       and you healed them all.
    Today we ask you to bless all those in sickness,
       in weakness and in pain;
       those who are blind and cannot see the light of the sun,
       the beauty of the world or the faces of their friends;
       those who are deaf and cannot hear the voices
       which speak to them;
       those who are immobile and confined to their homes.
    Bless all such people.

       Those whose minds have lost their reason;
       those who are so nervous they cannot cope with life;
       those who worry about everything.
    Bless all such people.

       Those whose weakness means they must always be careful;
       those whose disabilities mean that they cannot enter into
       the more strenuous activities or pleasures of life.
    Bless all such people.

    Grant that we in our health and our strength may never find those
       who are weak or disabled a nuisance,
       but grant that we may always do and give all that we can
       to see that they are included in the life of society.

William Barclay (1907-1978)

164   O loving Father,
    we pray for all who are disadvantaged on their journey of life;
       the blind,
       the sick in mind, body or spirit,
       and all who are disabled.
    We pray for those worn out with sickness
       and those who are wasted with unhappiness,
       for the dying and all unhappy children.
    May they learn the mystery of the road of suffering
       which Christ has trodden and the saints have followed,
       and bring you this gift which angels cannot bring:
       a heart that trusts you even in the dark.
    This we ask in the name of him who himself took
       our sorrows upon him,
       the same Jesus Christ.

A. S. T. Fisher

O God, the Father of all, 165
we commend to your ceaseless compassion
   all homeless children and orphans,
   and those whose lives are overshadowed by violence
   or thwarted by disease or cruelty.
Awaken in us your living love
   that we may not rest while children cry for bread
   or go uncomforted for lack of love.

The Mothers' Union Service Book

Open our eyes 166
   that they may see the deepest needs of men and women;
Move our hands
   that they may feed the hungry;
Touch our hearts
   that they may bring warmth to the despairing;
Teach us the generosity
   that welcomes strangers;
Let us share our possessions
   to clothe the naked;
Give us the care
   that strengthens the sick;
Make us share in the quest
   to set the prisoners free;
In sharing our anxiety and our love,
   our poverty and our prosperity,
   we partake of your divine presence.

Canaan Banana (b. 1936)

Gracious Father, we pray for your holy, Christian church. 167
Fill it with all truth, in all truth with all peace.
   Where it is corrupt, cleanse it.
   Where it is in error, direct it.
   Where it is superstitious, rectify it.
   Where anything is amiss, reform it.
   Where it is right, strengthen and confirm it.
   Where it is in want, supply its need.
   Where it is divided and torn apart, heal the divisions,
   O Holy One of Israel.

William Laud (1573-1645)

168 Lord, we thank you for our families.
May we treat one another with respect, honesty and care.
May we share the little discoveries and changes each day brings.
May we always try to be sensitive to one another's joys, sorrows,
  needs and changing moods,
and realise that being a loving family means not necessarily
  understanding everyone all the time,
but being there to love and help them just the same.

Author unknown

169 Be mindful of your church, O Lord.
  Deliver it from all evil,
  perfect it with your love,
  sanctify it,
  and gather it together from throughout the world
  into the kingdom which you have prepared for it.
For yours is the power and the glory for ever and ever.

The Didache

170 Guide and rule your church for ever, Lord,
  that it may walk warily in times of quiet
  and boldly in times of trouble;
  through our Lord Jesus Christ.

Franciscan Breviary

171 Look in mercy, heavenly Father,
  on this troubled and divided world.
Though we cannot always trace your footsteps
  or understand your working,
  give us grace to trust you
  with an undoubting faith.
And when the time you have set has come, Lord,
  show us the new heaven and the new earth,
  where righteousness lives
  and where the Prince of Peace rules,
  your Son, our Saviour Jesus Christ.

Charles John Vaughan (1816-1897)

Remember, O Lord, your church. 172
 Deliver it from evil and perfect it in your love.
 Strengthen and preserve it by your word and sacraments.
 Extend its influence,
  that your gospel may be preached to all nations.
Gather the faithful from throughout the world
 into the kingdom which you have prepared,
 through Jesus Christ our Lord.

Swedish Liturgy

Lord, 173
 the help of the helpless,
 the hope of those past hope,
 the rescuer of the storm-tossed,
 the harbour of the voyagers,
 the healer of the sick:
we ask you to become all things to all people,
 for you know the needs of each one.
Accept us all into your kingdom,
 making us children of light;
 and give us your peace and love,
 Lord our God.

Liturgy of St Basil (4th Century)

Give us, Lord God, a vision of the world 174
 as your love would make it:
a world where the weak are protected
 and none go hungry or poor;
a world where the benefits of civilised life
 are shared and everyone can enjoy them;
a world where different races, nations and cultures
 live in tolerance and mutual respect;
a world where peace is built with justice,
 and justice is guided by love;
and give us the inspiration and courage
to share in the task of building it,
through Jesus Christ our Lord.

Author unknown

175 Let the healing grace of your love, O Lord,
  so transform us that we may play our part in the
   transfiguration of the world
    from a place of suffering, death and corruption
    to a realm of infinite light, joy and love.
  Make us so obedient to your Spirit
   that our lives may become a living prayer,
   and a witness to your unfailing presence.

Martin Israel (b. 1927)

176 Lord Jesus, we praise and thank you
   that you have called and ordained servants
   within your church
   and set them apart for the ministry of word and sacrament.
  We pray that you will fill them with the fire of your love,
   that in their ministry they may be signs of
   your presence in the church.
  Since in themselves they are earthen vessels,
   we ask you to fill them with your power
   which shines in weakness.
  In sufferings, let them never be crushed;
   in doubt never despair;
   in temptation never be destroyed,
   in persecution never abandoned.
  Inspire them through prayer to live each day
   the mystery of your dying and rising.
  In times of weakness send them your Spirit,
   and help them to praise your heavenly Father
   and to pray for us.
  By your Spirit, put your word on their lips
   and your love in their hearts,
   to bring good news to the poor
   and healing to the broken hearted.
  And pour out that same Spirit upon the church,
   that together we may be signs
   of your sacrificial love in the world,
   to the glory of God the Father.

Author unknown

PRAYERS FOR THE WORLD, CHURCH AND PEOPLE

O God, who has bound us together in this bundle of life,   177
   give us grace to understand how all our lives depend
   on the courage, the work,
   the honesty and the integrity of others;
   so may we always be mindful of their needs,
   grateful for their faithfulness,
   and faithful in our responsibilities to them.

Reinhold Niebuhr (1892-1971)

Hear our humble prayer, O God, for all animals,   178
   especially those which are suffering:
   all that are overworked,
   underfed or otherwise cruelly treated;
   for all captive animals that long for freedom,
   and those that are hunted or lost,
   deserted, frightened or hungry.
We pray also for any creatures that are in pain or dying,
   and those that must be humanely destroyed out of kindness.
We ask that all who work with animals
   may have love in their hearts,
   gentleness in their hands
   and kind words on their lips.
Finally, help us to be kind and caring
   in all our dealings with animals
   and so to be the instrument of your compassion,
   for the sake of your Son who loves all creation,
   Jesus Christ our Lord.

Based on a Russian prayer

Lord of the future, the only ruler in eternity,   179
   set humankind free from the deadness of racial prejudice,
   nationalism and greed for power over others;
   enable the rich and powerful to find fulfilment
   in caring for the poor and weak;
   let the nations live together as one blood and fellowship,
   for you are brother to all humankind
   and by your blood we are set free from sin.

Richard Garrard (b. 1937)

180   Lord, we pray for all humankind.
Although divided into nations and races,
   yet all people are your children,
   drawing from you our daily life and our very being,
   commanded by you to obey your laws
   in accordance with our knowledge and understanding.
Help us to overcome strife and hatred,
   that lasting peace may fill the earth
   and humanity everywhere be blessed with the fruit of peace.
So shall the spirit of unity among all people
   show forth our faith that you are the Father of all.

Based on a Jewish Prayer

181   Our Father in heaven, we remember those
   whom in prayer we are inclined to forget.
We pray for those whom we dislike.
Defend us against our own feelings;
   change our inclinations;
   give us compassionate hearts.
Give us, we pray, the purity of heart
   which finds your image in all people.

J. H. Jowett (1864-1923)

182   Father of all, hear us
   when we pray for people of every race and nation.
May the light of your love break upon them,
   lightening their burdens
   and easing their anxieties.

Especially we pray for the marginalised
   and the neglected.
May our vision, and the vision of others,
   be increased that we become more aware
   of forgotten and unwanted people.
Help us so to order our lives
   and our societies
   that no-one is excluded.

Based on prayers by J. H. Jowett (1864-1923)

Lord Jesus, poorest of the poor,   183
   born in a borrowed stable
   and buried in a borrowed tomb,
we bring before you all those who, like you,
   have nowhere to lay their head:
   the war refugees exiled from their homes,
   migrants searching for a place to live,
   the victims of earthquakes, floods and disasters,
   and the countless, countless homeless in this land.
Help us, living as we are securely and in peace,
   to show compassion for our brothers and sisters,
   and to help them find in their lives
   a new beginning and new hope,
   for your name's sake.

H. J. Richards (b. 1921)

Eternal Father,   184
source of life and light,
whose love extends to all people,
all creatures, all things,
   grant us that reverence for life
   which becomes those who believe in you;
   lest we despise it, degrade it,
   or come callously to destroy it.
Rather, let us save it,
   secure it and sanctify it,
   after the example of your Son
   Jesus Christ our Lord.

Robert Runcie (b. 1921)

Lord Jesus, be near to all young children,   185
   that in the vulnerability and confusion,
   which this age can cause their growing personalities,
   they may come to no harm by the influence of adults;
   and grant to parents such sure knowledge of your love
   that they may guide their children with courage and faith.

New Every Morning

186 Lord,
  we pray for all those whose lives have touched ours,
   for good or evil,
   in the past or in the present,
   whether they are alive or departed.
  Give them an abundance of your grace in this world,
   and in eternity may they find joy in your presence,
   in the name of Jesus the Lord.

Alan Rees OSB (b. 1941)

187 Lord, make the old tolerant,
  the young sympathetic,
  the great humble,
  the busy patient.
 Make rich people understanding
  strong people gentle,
  those who are weak prayerful.
 Make the religious lovable,
  happy folk thoughtful,
  the clever kindly,
  the bad good,
  the good pleasant,
 and, dear Lord,
  make us what we ought to be.

Author unknown

188 Be pleased, O Lord, to remember our friends,
  all who have prayed for us,
  and all who have been good to us.
 Do good to them,
  and return all their kindness twofold,
  rewarding them with blessings,
  sanctifying them with your grace,
  and bringing them to glory.

Jeremy Taylor (1613-1667)

O God, we are one with you. 189
You have made us one with you.
You have taught us that if we are open to one another
  you dwell in us.
Help us to preserve this openness
  and to fight for it with all our hearts.
Help us to realise that there can be no understanding
  where there is mutual rejection.
O God, in accepting one another
wholeheartedly, fully, completely,
  we accept you,
  and we thank you,
  and we adore you,
  and we love you with our whole being,
  because our being is in your being,
  our spirit is rooted in your spirit.
Fill us then with love,
  and let us be bound together with love
  as we go our diverse ways united in this one spirit
  which makes you present in the world,
  and which makes you witness
  to the ultimate reality that is love.

Love has overcome.

Love is victorious.

Thomas Merton (1915-1968)

O God the Father, 190
  source of all that is good and true,
  in whom is calmness, peace and harmony,
  heal the dissensions which divide people from each other,
  and bring us back to a unity of love
  which may bear some likeness to your divine nature.
And as you are above all things,
  make us one by unity of thought,
  that through the bonds of love we may be one,
  both with ourselves and with each other;
  through that peace of yours which makes all things peaceful,
  and through the grace, mercy and love of your Son,
  Jesus Christ.

St Dionysius (6th Century)

191 Dear Lord, you have sent us into this world
        to preach your word.
    So often the problems of the world seem
        so complex and intricate
        that your word strikes us as embarrassingly simple.
    Many times we feel tongue-tied in the company of people
        who are dealing with the world's
        social and economic problems.

    But you, O Lord, said, 'Be clever as serpents
        and innocent as doves'.
    Let us retain innocence and simplicity
        in the midst of this complex world.
    We realise that we have to be informed,
        that we have to study the many aspects of the
        problems facing the world,
        and that we have to try to understand as fully as possible
        the dynamics of our contemporary society.
    But what really counts is that all this information,
        knowledge and insight
        allows us to speak your truthful word
        more clearly and unambiguously.
    Do not allow evil powers to seduce us with the
        complexity of the world's problems,
        but give us the strength to think clearly,
        speak freely and act boldly in your service.
    Give us the courage to show the dove
        in a world so full of serpents.

Henri Nouwen (b.1932)

192 Lord, open our eyes,
        that we may see you in our brothers and sisters.
    Lord, open our ears,
        that we may hear the cries of the hungry,
        the cold, the frightened and the oppressed.
    Lord, open our hearts,
        that we may love each other as you love us.
    Renew in us your spirit, Lord,
        free us and make us one.

Mother Teresa (b. 1910)

Teach us, Lord, to hope in you, 193
    for you are the source and fount of all creation.
Open our hearts to know you
    who alone are the highest and most holy.
Grant us, Lord, your help and protection.
    Save the afflicted, raise the fallen,
    reveal yourself to the needy, heal the sick,
    and bring home your wandering people.
    Feed the hungry, set free the captive,
    support the weak, comfort the faint-hearted.
Most merciful Lord,
    forgive us our sins and offences,
    our errors and shortcomings.
    Do not hold our sins against us,
    but make us clean.
Guide us in all that we do,
    so that we may walk in holiness of heart,
    and our actions may be pleasing in your sight.
Show us the light of your face in peace;
    shelter us by your mighty hand,
    and save us from all wrongdoing by your outstretched arm.
Give to us, and to all people, peace and harmony.
    Make us obedient to your almighty and glorious name
    and give us a proper regard for those in authority on earth.
    Grant to them health, peace and security,
    that they may exercise, and not abuse
    whatever authority you have given them.
To you, who alone can supply these and all good things,
    we offer our praises through Jesus Christ,
    the high priest and guardian of our souls.
Through him be glory and majesty to you
    now and for all generations through all ages.

St Clement of Rome (d. c.100)

Father, 194
your own Son did not refuse to be born
    in the very thick of our muddle.
Humbly imitating him,
    may we show to your world
    the new life by which we are transformed.

Carmelite Monastery, Quidenham

195 O God our Father, we give you thanks
>that today you have called us to worship you
>and to learn of you.
You know the needs with which we have come to your house.
Grant that in it we may find comfort for sorrow,
>and soothing for soreness of heart.
Grant that in it we may find guidance for problems
>and light for perplexity of mind.
Grant that in it we may find strength against our temptations
>and grace to overcome the fascination of the wrong things.
Grant that in it we may meet Jesus,
>and go out not to forget him any more.
Remember those who cannot go to church today:
>those who are ill;
>those who are aged;
>those who are too sad to come;
>those who have the care of children
>and of family concerns;
>those who are nursing invalids;
>those who must work even today.
And grant that in their own home,
>in the hospitals,
>the infirmaries,
>the nursing homes,
they may know the unseen fellowship
>of the worshipping company
>of those who love you.

William Barclay (1907-1978)

196 Strengthen us, Lord, to face the task,
>the crucifying task,
>of being reconcilers amongst guilt and fear,
>anxiety and anger.
Bring us, Lord, further to the point
>where we can accept life,
>with all its problems and pains,
>with gladness and exultation,
>not because of future perks in a future heaven,
>but because we know that to be fully human we can do no other.

Rex Chapman (b. 1938)

197

You, O God, are the Lord of the mountains and valleys.
You are our mother and our father.
You have given us rain to make the corn grow,
   and sunshine to ripen it.
Now in your strength the harvest begins.

We offer you the first morsels of the harvest.
We know it is almost nothing compared with
   the abundance of the crop.
But since you have provided the harvest,
   our gifts to you are only a sign of what you have given to us.

You alone know how many suns and moons
   it will take to finish reaping.
You alone know how heavy the crop will be.
If we work too hard and too fast
   we forget about you who gave us the harvest.
So we will work steadily and slowly,
   remembering that each ear of corn
   is a priceless gift from you.

A Sioux prayer

Prayers for Morning & Evening

Our Father in heaven, 198
    teach us the value of little things.
Show us how to consecrate what seems insignificant,
    and to recognise the light of your presence in every moment.
May we glorify the day by offering
    each minute to be redeemed by your love.
We offer you all our moments.

J. H. Jowett (1864-1923)

Thank you, Lord, for this brand new day. 199
Give us the wisdom to see its possibilities,
    the strength to face its challenges,
    and the grace to be open to its promise.
Give us your heart of love to do a favour,
    speak a kindness, offer a hand,
    soothe a hurt, celebrate a joy,
    share a sorrow, or in some small way
    give of ourselves in love to others
    in your name.

Author unknown

Lord, for today, 200
we simply pray that we may love and be loved;
    that we may serve as you served;
    that we may give ourselves for our brothers and sisters.
Today, we pray that we may share your word in the
    power of the Spirit as opportunity presents itself,
    and that we may never be held back by human respect or fear.
Give us the spirit of prayer
    and of continued thanksgiving in all circumstances of life,
    especially in the difficult ones.
Heal us, Lord,
    and grant us simplicity and unity within ourselves,
    through Jesus Christ the Lord.

Alan Rees OSB (b. 1941)

201   Take all hate from our hearts, O God,
       and teach us how to take it from the hearts of others.
    Open our eyes and show us what things in our society
       make it easy for hatred to flourish
       and hard for us to conquer it.
    Then help us to try to change these things.
    And so open our eyes and our hearts
       that we may this coming day be able
       to do some work of peace for you.

Alan Paton (1903-1988)

202   Our Father, may this day bring us new vision,
       new sense of responsibility,
       new consciousness of the joy of being
       your children.
    Draw us into closer communion with you,
       and make us partners in your love,
       your joy,
       your rest,
       your peace.

J. H. Jowett (1864-1923)

203   O Lord, enable us to greet the coming day in peace.
    Help us in all things to rely upon your holy will.
    Throughout the day reveal your will to us.
    Bless our dealings with all who surround us.
    Teach us to treat all that comes to us
       throughout the day with peace of soul
       and with firm conviction that your purpose
       is at work in all things.
    Guide our thoughts and feelings,
       our words and actions.
    In unforeseen events,
       let us not lose sight of your presence.
    Teach us to act firmly and wisely,
       without embittering and embarrassing others.
    Give us strength to bear whatever stress
       the coming day may bring.
    Direct our wills,
       teach us to pray,
       and let your Holy Spirit pray in us.

Metropolitan Philaret of Moscow (1782-1867)

Arising from sleep,   204
we fall down before you,
O blessed God,
and join in the angelic hymn:
    Holy, holy, holy are you, O God.
    Have mercy upon us, we pray.

Eastern Orthodox

O Lord, when we awake and day begins,   205
    waken us to your presence;
    waken us to your indwelling Spirit;
    waken us to inward sight of you,
    and speech with you,
    and strength from you;
that all our earthly walk may waken into song
    and our spirits leap up to you all day,
    all ways.

Eric Milner-White (1884-1964)

Into your hands, heavenly Father,   206
    we place this new day.
You know how wayward we are;
    you know how quickly our thoughts stray from you
    and from Jesus, the way, the truth and the life.
We ask you to give us your Holy Spirit
    in good measure this day;
    may he be our guide.
May he govern every detail of our lives,
    however small and insignificant.
May he fill us with love and praise,
    so that every moment of this day may belong to you.
Without you, O holy and blessed Trinity,
    our lives lack purpose,
    but filled with the gift of the Holy Spirit
    they take on the dimension of your glory.
Stay with us, great God,
    and enable us to live for the praise of your glory.
We ask this in Jesus' name.

Alan Rees OSB (b. 1941)

207   Help us to remember, Lord God,
       that every day is your gift
          and ought to be used according to your will.

Samuel Johnson (1709-1784)

208   Lord, you are always with us.
       No weakness can keep you away,
          no besetting sin.
       In all seasons,
          at all times,
          you are with us,
          until we meet again
          in your kingdom.

Graham Jeffery (b. 1935)

209   Save us, O Lord, while we are awake,
         and guard us while we sleep,
           that awake we may watch with Christ,
           and asleep we may rest in peace,
           in Jesus' name.

The Office of Compline

210   Lord Jesus, heal us of the wounds of yesterday
         that we may live abundantly today
       and with confidence in your Providence
         go forward into tomorrow.

Alan Rees OSB (b. 1941)

Our Father, on this new day 211
    may we experience your great renewal.
May our duties, our sympathies,
    our aspirations be renewed.
May we experience a new heaven
    and a new earth.

J. H. Jowett (1864-1923)

O God, we humbly pray that you will 212
    purify our hearts from all vain,
    worldly and sinful thoughts,
    and so prepare our souls to worship you well today
    with reverence and holy awe.
Focus our attention on things above, all the day long,
    and give us grace to receive your word
        into honest and open hearts,
    and bear fruit with patience.

Gavin Hamilton (1561-1612)

Thank you, Lord, for this new day. 213
Thank you for the people you will put in our way:
    people wounded by life,
    by sin, by others;
    broken people created by you for love
        but not experiencing it.
Thank you for them.
Let us never add to their burden, to their grief.

Use us for them,
    if only in a smile and an encouraging word
        to bring them life and light.
Let us live in the truth today, Lord;
    let your truth become our truth
    and please set us free in the process.
Let us abide in you and let your word,
    your will, become our home.

Alan Rees OSB (b. 1941)

214   Help us, O God, to serve you and your world well today
May we do our work carefully,
    help others without indulging in ostentation,
    enjoy your gifts of food and drink,
    but without vulgarity or excess,
    and be a good friend to others.
Then may we go to bed contented and sleep well,
through Jesus Christ our Lord.

Based on a Medieval prayer

215   We unite and submit our will to yours
    in every event of this day
    however unpleasant,
    happy or boring.
We will try not to be cast down by blame,
    failure, weakness and loneliness,
    nor elated by praise and success.
Keep our souls in peace with you, Lord,
    and our bodies relaxed and free of tension.

Alan Rees OSB (b. 1941)

216   Lord Jesus Christ,
    who very early in the morning
    while the sun was still rising,
    rose from the dead:
raise us up daily to newness of life,
    and save us,
    for you are our Lord and Saviour.

Lancelot Andrewes (1555-1625)

PRAYERS FOR MORNING AND EVENING

O Lord,   217
    support us all through the long day of our lives,
    until the shadows lengthen
    and the evening comes,
    and the busy world is hushed,
    and the fever of life over,
    and our work is done.
Then, Lord, in your mercy,
    grant us a safe lodging,
    a holy rest,
    and peace at the last.

John Henry Newman (1801-1890)

Watch, dear Lord,   218
    with those who wake, or watch, or weep tonight,
    and give your angels charge over those who sleep.
Tend your sick ones, O Lord Christ,
    rest your weary ones,
    bless your dying ones,
    soothe your suffering ones,
    pity your afflicted ones,
    shield your joyous ones.
We ask all this for your love's sake.

St Augustine of Hippo (354-430)

We thank you, Lord,   219
    that you have kept us through this day.
We thank you, Lord,
    that you will keep us through the night.
Bring us in safety, Lord,
    to the morning hours,
    that you may receive our praise at all times,
    through Jesus Christ our Lord.

Gelasian Sacramentary (6th Century)

220   Eternal and ever-blessed God,
we give you thanks, as the day comes to an end,
    for those who mean so much to us
    and without whom life could never be the same.

We thank you for those to whom we can go at any time
    and never feel a nuisance.

We thank you for those to whom we can go when we are tired,
    knowing that they have,
    for weary feet,
    the gift of rest.

We thank you for those with whom we can talk,
    and keep nothing back,
    knowing that they will not laugh at our dreams
    or mock our failures.

We thank you for those in whose presence
    it is easier to be good.

We thank you for those in whose company joys are increased
    and sorrow's bitterness is soothed.

We thank you for those who by their timely warning and
    their criticism
    have helped us avoid mistakes we might have made
    and sins we might have committed.

And above all,
we thank you for Jesus,
    the pattern for our lives,
    the Lord of our hearts
    and the Saviour of our souls.

Accept this our thanksgiving,
    and grant us tonight a good night's rest;
    through Jesus Christ our Lord.

William Barclay (1907-1978)

221   Lighten our darkness, Lord, we pray,
    and in your great mercy defend us from
    all perils and dangers of this night,
    for the sake of your only Son,
    our Saviour Jesus Christ.

Gelasian Sacramentary (6th Century)

O Lord our God, 222
    forgive us the sins we have committed this day
    in thought, word or deed,
    for you are gracious and you love all people.
Grant us peaceful, undisturbed sleep;
    send your guardian angel
    to protect and guard us from every evil,
    for you are the guardian of our souls and bodies,
    and to you is ascribed glory,
    Father, Son and Holy Spirit,
    now and for ever.

Russian Orthodox

Lord Jesus Christ, Saviour and Redeemer, 223
we ask you to be Lord of our sleep;
    be Lord of our resting and of our rising;
    be Lord of our dreams.
Do not let the evil one approach us in the hours of sleep.
Breathe the gentle breath of the Holy Spirit
    into our hearts during these hours of unconsciousness;
    even while we sleep let him be our teacher and guide.
Speak your word to our hearts
    – words of peace and consolation.
Lift us up into the Father's arms,
    way above the cares and anxieties,
    the temptations and sufferings of this life;
    way above the snares and deceits of the devil.
Let us rest surrounded by the Father's love,
    secure in the salvation won for us
    by your precious blood,
    and abiding in the resurrection joy
    through the power of the Holy Spirit.
We make this prayer in your name, Jesus,
    for to you, together with the eternal Father
    and the life giving Spirit,
    belong all power, glory,
    might, majesty and praise.
Amen. Alleluia.

Alan Rees OSB (b. 1941)

224   Be present, O merciful God,
        and protect us through the silent hours of this night,
        so that we who are wearied by the changes
        and chances of this fleeting world
        may rest upon your eternal changelessness;
        through Jesus Christ our Lord.

The Office of Compline

225   O Lord our God, thank you
        for bringing this day to a close.
    Thank you for giving us rest
        in body and in soul.
    Your hand has been over us
        and has guarded and preserved us.
    Forgive our lack of faith,
        and any wrong that we have done today,
        and help us to forgive all who have wronged us.
    Let us sleep in peace under your protection,
        and keep us from all the temptations of darkness.
    Into your hands we commend our loved ones;
    we commend to you our bodies and souls.
    O God, may your holy name be praised.

Dietrich Bonhoeffer (1906-1945)

Prayers of Blessing & Commendation

PRAYERS OF BLESSING AND COMMENDATION

Into your hands, O Father and Lord,   226
we commend our souls and bodies,
   our parents and homes,
   our families, friends and neighbours,
   all people of faith and love,
   and all who stand in special need.
Lighten our lives with your holy grace
   and the knowledge of your constant presence,
O Lord in Trinity, God everlasting.

St Edmund of Abingdon (c.1175-1240)

Bless us, God the Father,   227
   you who have created us.
Bless us, God the Son,
   you who have set us free.
Bless us, God the Holy Spirit,
   you who make us holy.
O blessed Trinity, keep us in body,
   soul and spirit, to life eternal.

'Weimarischer Gesangbuch' (1873)

Father, we surrender ourselves into your hands;   228
   do with us what you will.
Whatever you may do,
   we accept with thanks.
We are prepared.
Let your will alone be done in us
   and in all your creatures.
We wish no more than this, O Lord.

Into your hands we commend our souls.
We offer them to you with the love of all our hearts,
   for we love you, Lord,
   and so need to give ourselves,
   to surrender ourselves into your hands without reserve,
   and with boundless confidence,
   for you are our Father.

Charles de Foucauld (1858-1916)

229 May the peace of God,
        which surpasses all understanding,
        keep our hearts and minds
        in the knowledge and love of God,
        and of his Son, the Lord Jesus Christ:
     and may the blessing of God almighty,
        Father, Son and Holy Spirit,
        be with us and all whom we love,
        now and always.

Adapted from the Book of Common Prayer

230 Deep peace of the running wave to you,
        deep peace of the flowing air to you,
        deep peace of the quiet earth to you,
        deep peace of the shining stars to you,
        deep peace of the Son of Peace to you.

Celtic Benediction

231 Take us to yourself, Lord,
        that we may truly live.
     We know that you will do all things for us;
        you will never disappoint us.

Carmelite Monastery, Quidenham

232 May the grace of the Lord Jesus Christ,
        the love of God
        and the fellowship of the Holy Spirit
        be with us evermore.

Based on 2 Corinthians 13:13

PRAYERS OF BLESSING AND COMMENDATION

Lord Jesus Christ,   233
we praise and thank you for those closest to us
   whom you have given to us to cherish.
Surround them with your tender loving care,
   teach them to love and serve one another in true affection
   and to look to you in all their needs.
We place them all in your care,
   knowing that your love for them is greater than our own.
Keep us close to one another in this life
   and conduct us at the last to our true and heavenly home.
Blessed be God for ever.

Author unknown

Holy God, we place ourselves in your hands.   234
   Bless us and care for us,
   be gracious and loving to us;
   look kindly upon us and give us peace.

Based on the Aaronic blessing: Numbers 6:24-26

God the Father, bless us;   235
Jesus Christ, take care of us;
Holy Spirit, enlighten us all the days of our lives.
O Lord, be our defender and keeper,
   both now and for ever, through all ages.

Aedelwald, Saxon Bishop, 9th Cent.

May the rich blessing of the Lord be with us,   236
   and forgive our sins.
May the Lord graciously protect us from all evil
   and keep us in all good.
May he who created and redeemed us
   keep us for himself without blemish to the end.

Mozarabic Sacramentary (3rd Century)

237	We commend to you, O God,
    our souls and our bodies,
    our minds and our thoughts,
    our prayers and our hopes,
    our health and our work,
    our life and our death,
    our relatives and our friends,
    our neighbours and fellow citizens,
    and all people,
    this day and always.

Lancelot Andrewes (1555-1626)

238	May the strength of God lead us,
    may the power of God preserve us,
    may the wisdom of God instruct us,
    may the hand of God protect us,
    may the way of God direct us,
    may the shield of God defend us,
    may the hosts of God guard us
    against the snares of evil
    and the temptations of the world.
May your salvation, O Lord, always be ours
    this day and for evermore.

St Patrick (349-461)

239	Bless your servants
    with health of body and of spirit.
Let the hand of your blessing
    be upon our heads night and day,
    and support us in every need,
    strengthen us in temptations,
    comfort us in all sorrows,
    and let us be your servants in all circumstances;
    and help us both to live with you for ever in your favour,
    and in the light of your face,
    and in your glory.

Jeremy Taylor (1613-1667)

Indices

The Day at Prayer

The beginning of the day
1, 7, 17, 34, 36, 39, 45, 59, 63, 64, 69, 92, 111, 113, 117, 123, 150, 160, 162, 163, 192, 198, 199, 200, 201, 202, 203, 204, 205, 206, 207, 210, 211, 212, 213, 215, 216, 229, 233, 236, 239

At work
17, 23, 27, 30, 34, 36, 46, 94, 101, 102, 198

Encountering others
14, 22, 23, 32, 34, 35, 49, 50, 59, 62, 69, 94, 111, 113, 160, 162, 199, 200, 201, 213, 239

In relaxation
30, 36, 46, 198, 223, 230

Meal times
43, 53

The end of the day
4, 7, 51, 67, 68, 133, 135, 140, 143, 144, 146, 165, 186, 188, 209, 217, 218, 219, 220, 221, 222, 223, 224, 226, 228, 230, 232, 234, 235

The Year at Prayer

Advent
2, 9, 13, 159

Christmas
6, 21, 70, 116, 125, 161, 165, 194, 208

Lent
25, 37, 41, 46, 51, 62, 74, 76, 77, 88, 89, 90, 96, 98, 100, 117, 119, 123, 132, 158, 190, 193, 222

Passiontide
30, 57, 61, 66, 74, 75, 79, 84, 85, 87, 98, 129, 137, 138, 164, 196

Easter
47, 70, 83, 92, 105, 116, 134, 211

Pentecost
1, 3, 12, 13, 63, 72, 78, 95, 105, 167, 170, 172, 176, 180

Harvest
64, 75, 157, 197

One World Week
13, 23, 45, 49, 51, 57, 60, 79, 80, 84, 85, 89, 91, 100, 110, 111, 113, 116, 117, 120, 122, 128, 142, 148, 151, 154, 156, 190, 201, 213

Week of Prayer for Christian Unity
29, 31, 56, 69, 74, 80, 89, 105, 106, 113, 117, 122, 158, 159, 167, 169, 170, 172, 189, 190, 196

On holiday
35, 36, 39, 50, 51, 53, 54, 60, 128, 135, 152, 155, 157, 159, 160, 161, 162, 163, 165, 166, 174, 175, 177, 179, 180, 182, 183, 184, 191, 192, 196, 197, 198, 202

Back to work/school
23, 27, 30, 34, 36, 59, 65, 102, 110, 117, 123, 139, 156, 198, 200, 203, 238

Birthdays and anniversaries
25, 36, 53, 67, 124, 135, 140, 169, 185, 202, 211, 217, 233, 239

New Year
1, 3, 17, 29, 174

Sunday - Before worship
4, 8, 9, 10, 11, 12, 16, 17, 20, 24, 38, 43, 56, 104, 108, 126, 141, 195, 212

Sunday - After worship
14, 15, 18, 26, 31, 48, 118, 120, 127, 226, 237, 238

Index of Subjects

Acceptance
27, 35, 36, 40, 43, 49, 97, 98, 100, 102, 106, 109, 112, 132, 133, 147, 168, 190, 203, 212, 215, 228

Anxiety
36, 59, 78, 79, 93, 97, 106, 109, 132, 136, 137, 138, 142, 156, 210, 218, 221

Assurance
5, 7, 20, 36, 42, 61, 70, 71, 74, 75, 76, 114, 130, 132, 140, 185, 208, 217, 219, 223, 233

Communion of Saints
4, 44, 74, 186

Compassion
3, 11, 45, 60, 110, 113, 114, 116, 118, 125, 128, 149, 153, 157, 160, 161, 162, 163, 165, 166, 181, 182, 183, 199, 213

Contentment
2, 21, 23, 30, 32, 43, 45, 46, 48, 49, 98, 100, 102, 112, 117, 190, 198, 200, 203

Courage
12, 21, 27, 59, 79, 111, 117, 119, 122, 132, 135, 142, 158, 160, 174, 177, 191, 196, 210

Creation
1, 13, 57, 60, 61, 63, 64, 69, 97, 152, 178, 184, 197, 230

Darkness
74, 76, 83, 92, 106, 113, 119, 125, 136, 138, 142, 143, 151, 164, 217, 218, 221, 224

Death and dying
4, 44, 136, 137, 162, 175, 217, 218, 231

Doubt
3, 122, 137, 138

Encouragement
5, 74, 105, 144, 170, 176, 191, 193, 210, 213

Eternal life
13, 19, 20, 42, 43, 44, 74, 83, 113, 125, 126, 142, 143, 171, 186, 188, 216, 217, 227, 231, 233

Faith
25, 74, 87, 90, 97, 99, 105, 106, 109, 119, 122, 132, 225

Forgiveness
79. 80, 84, 85, 86, 88, 89, 90, 93, 96, 113, 140, 147, 181, 193, 196, 222, 225

Friendship
32, 35, 44, 49, 56, 105, 115, 133, 154, 177, 188, 199, 203, 220, 233

Gifts
42, 45, 49, 57, 68, 72, 75, 106, 117, 128

Gifts of the Holy Spirit
1, 78, 87, 90, 95, 135, 159

Grace
3, 8, 31, 33, 49, 50, 58, 66, 67, 69, 72, 75, 76, 78, 81, 84, 94, 95, 99, 100, 103, 106, 108, 119, 123, 124, 126, 127, 129, 131, 137, 141, 150, 158, 167, 170, 187, 188, 191, 195, 196, 199, 201, 205, 211, 217, 226, 227, 232

Growing
27, 40, 41, 42, 44, 50, 58, 60, 95, 98, 132, 149, 185, 203

Guidance
22, 23, 29, 82, 99, 101, 103, 107, 109, 115, 125, 131, 134, 135, 142, 158, 170, 185, 193, 203, 206, 223, 233

Healing
8, 20, 57, 83, 84, 96, 110, 113, 114, 116, 118, 137, 144, 147, 148, 151, 152, 159, 163, 165, 166, 167, 173, 175, 179, 193, 195, 200, 210, 220

Holy Communion
8, 20, 31, 43, 104, 141, 195

Hope
18, 46, 51, 74, 87, 90, 93, 105, 113, 114, 129, 136, 137, 138, 141, 156, 158, 164, 175, 193, 216, 217

Humility
3, 15, 21, 35, 41, 45, 89, 92, 94, 102, 109, 117, 122, 139

Inspiration
12, 17, 24, 37, 39, 40, 58, 63, 64, 72, 74, 79, 92, 116, 122, 124, 127, 141, 152, 159, 194, 211, 213

INDICES

Journey of Life
43, 74, 99, 101, 107, 119, 130, 131, 135, 136, 161, 164, 173, 205, 233

Joy
10, 37, 49, 51, 55, 63, 65, 70, 95, 137, 162, 175, 186, 196

Justice
49, 57, 69, 78, 79, 84, 85, 100, 111, 116, 148, 152, 153, 155, 159, 164, 171, 173, 174, 175, 180, 191, 194, 213, 218
homelessness
128, 160, 165, 166, 183, 192
hunger
45, 128, 157, 162, 166, 174, 182, 192, 193
oppression
60, 80, 84, 128, 148, 151, 159, 160, 161, 165, 166, 174, 179, 182, 183, 192, 193
poverty
45, 80, 148, 151, 156, 157, 160, 162, 166, 174, 179, 182, 183, 193
prejudice
29, 60, 94, 154, 159, 174, 177, 179, 180, 182, 189, 192, 201

Kindness
84, 89, 110, 113, 114, 116, 118, 121, 151, 162, 165, 166, 168, 178, 187, 188, 193, 199, 213, 220

Kingdom of God
32, 51, 54, 77, 80, 91, 104, 106, 111, 152, 154, 158, 159, 160, 161, 162, 166, 167, 169, 171, 172, 173, 174, 175, 176, 179, 180, 182, 184, 189, 191, 194, 233

Light
6, 11, 14, 20, 65, 83, 92, 106, 113, 136, 142, 143, 153, 173, 175, 216, 226

Loneliness
76, 97, 110, 119, 136, 145, 161, 182, 215

Love
of God
33, 37, 43, 78, 85, 87, 95, 100, 105, 118, 125, 140, 149, 154, 159, 161, 163, 165, 166, 173, 174, 175, 179, 185, 189, 192, 218, 232, 233
for God
25, 28, 72, 81, 87, 90, 95, 106, 108, 134, 150, 157, 160, 189
for each other
15, 31, 32, 49, 52, 56, 72, 78, 87, 90, 91, 95, 100, 105, 106, 110, 113, 118, 149, 154, 155, 157, 158, 159, 160, 161, 162, 165, 166, 175, 180, 183, 185, 189, 192, 199, 200, 220, 233

Marriage and family
53, 56, 168, 177, 186, 189, 220, 233, 239

Mercy
11, 68, 76, 96, 125, 144, 145, 147, 193, 217, 218

Mystery
5, 8, 12, 16, 20, 26, 31, 39, 51, 61, 64, 87, 96, 119, 122, 125, 138

Offering and giving
48, 57, 97, 98, 100, 104, 106, 107, 108, 125, 129, 133, 197, 198, 199, 228

Patience
26, 46, 74, 78, 89, 102, 106, 123, 142, 176, 203, 210, 212

Peace
18, 31, 45, 54, 56, 78, 84, 85, 92, 94, 99, 109, 111, 118, 130, 132, 135, 137, 142, 147, 152, 154, 160, 161, 162, 173, 174, 177, 179, 180, 182, 183, 189, 191, 192, 196, 215, 217, 222, 224, 229, 230, 234

Power
11, 12, 21, 37, 45, 94, 185, 191, 193, 238

Prayer
17, 47, 56, 107, 119, 126, 142, 175, 181, 203, 204, 205, 212

Presence of God
3, 5, 10, 13, 14, 18, 37, 42, 44, 48, 63, 64, 71, 76, 98, 101, 116, 119, 125, 131, 132, 134, 136, 137, 140, 143, 144, 147, 148, 151, 157, 159, 160, 164, 166, 170, 179, 181, 183, 185, 186, 189, 194, 195, 203, 205, 206, 208, 209, 213, 217, 219, 222, 223, 224, 226, 229, 231, 232, 233, 235, 238

Protection
4, 7, 18, 25, 32, 54, 96, 103, 135, 142, 193, 209, 218, 219, 221, 222, 223, 224, 225, 226, 227, 234, 235, 236, 238

Providence
5, 8, 32, 43, 45, 49, 64, 66, 68, 70, 71, 73, 75, 76, 97, 116, 118, 130, 148, 151, 165, 167, 173, 190, 193, 197, 210, 219, 220, 231

Purity
13, 22, 24, 31, 33, 37, 52, 144, 181, 193, 212

121

Redemption
31, 57, 61, 66, 69, 79, 84, 85, 87, 104, 129, 137, 138, 223, 236

Salvation
4, 8, 20, 31, 33, 66, 68, 69, 73, 83, 87, 142, 144, 196, 216, 217, 220, 222, 223, 236, 238

Service
15, 28, 34, 41, 45, 59, 60, 77, 81, 97, 102, 104, 110, 112, 115, 116, 117, 121, 123, 124, 127, 128, 133, , 153, 157, 158, 162, 163, 166, 183, 196, 197, 200, 201, 202, 213

Simplicity
21, 40, 45, 46, 47, 48, 49, 51, 53, 63, 64, 80, 98, 106, 108, 109, 120, 130, 132, 198, 230

Solitude
119, 137

Stillness
23, 36, 51, 54, 63, 126, 132, 139, 147, 149, 202

Stress
3, 41, 51, 99, 102, 109, 130, 132, 135, 139, 145, 147, 202, 203, 217

Success and failure
30, 49, 79, 97, 102, 105, 111, 123, 129, 140, 146, 151, 215

Temptation
23, 126, 132, 135, 195, 225, 238

Time
36, 42, 53, 64, 74, 75, 102, 126, 146, 179, 186, 198, 200, 205, 206, 207, 208, 210, 213, 220, 224, 225

Trinity
80, 88, 105, 119, 125, 149, 206, 222, 223, 226, 227, 229, 232, 235

Truth
22, 29, 31, 33, 42, 62, 63, 65, 73, 74, 77, 82, 91, 103, 117, 122, 126, 127, 131, 158, 167, 174, 191, 213, 220

Vision
10, 16, 19, 29, 57, 58, 59, 63, 64, 74, 91, 103, 116, 122, 125, 132, 135, 152, 153, 154, 170, 174, 181, 182, 192, 201, 202, 211

Waiting and watching
9, 26, 46, 137, 145

Wisdom
1, 11, 21, 26, 27, 29, 65, 73, 124, 185, 191, 199, 238

Witness
12, 14, 26, 64, 77, 105, 115, 194, 200, 220

Work
17, 36, 102, 107, 117, 123, 126, 156, 177, 185, 197

Index of Authors and Sources

A
2 Corinthians 13:13, 232
à Kempis, Thomas, 29, 92, 104
Abu Bekr, 62
Aedelwald, 235
Albrecht, Bernard, 142
Alcuin, 11
Alford, Henry, 100
Alfred, King, 65
Alphonsus Liguori, St, 81
Andrewes, Lancelot, 216, 237
Anselm, St, 39, 148
Appleton, George, 69
Augustine of Hippo, St, 28, 37, 218

B
Banana, Canaan, 166
Barclay, William, 89, 163, 195, 220
Basil of Caesarea, St, 43, 135
Benedict, St, 17, 26
Benson, Edward, 102
Bonaventure, St, 18
Bonhoeffer, Dietrich, 225
Book of Common Prayer, 229
Bullivant, A. G., 35

C
Carmelite Monastery, Quidenham, 2, 7, 10, 42, 70, 93, 145, 194, 231
Catherine of Sienna, 61
Catholic Prayer Book (1970), 22
Celtic, 230
Chapman, Rex, 196
Clement of Rome, St, 193
Compline, Office of, 209, 224
Coptic Liturgy of St Cyril, 52
Cosin, John, 75

D
de Foucauld, Charles, 228
Dewey, Margaret, 36
Didache, 169
Dionysius, St, 190

E
Eastern, 94
Eastern Orthodox, 13, 67, 85, 94, 204
Edmund of Abingdon, 124, 226

F
Fellowship Litanies, 74
Fisher, A. S. T., 164
Francis of Assisi, St, 113
Franciscan Breviary, 170

G
Garrard, Richard, 57, 179
Gelasian Sacramentary, 33, 54, 219, 221
Grail Prayer, 107

H
Hamilton, Gavin, 212
Hare, Maria, 99
Hindu Scriptures, 56
How, William Walsham, 77
Hume, Basil, 155
Hunt, Jenny, 51

I
Ignatius Loyola, St, 108, 112
Industrial Christian Fellowship, 156
Israel, Martin, 175

J
Jeffery, Graham, 40, 129, 134, 138, 140, 146, 152, 208
Jewish, 180
John 15:9-11, 55
John XXII, Pope, 4
John XXIII, Pope, 128
Johnson, Samuel, 207
Jowett, J. H., 30, 38, 60, 63, 139, 181, 182, 198, 202, 211

K
Ken, Thomas, 32
Kenyan Prayer, 117
Kerr, Cecil, 159
Kingsley, Charles, 21
Knight, William Angus, 49, 151
Kontakion (Eastern Orthodox), 72

L
Laud, William, 167
Leighton, Robert, 82
Leonine Sacramentary, 19
Liturgical Institute, Trier, 15
Liturgy of Malabar, 31
Liturgy of St. Basil, 173

M
Manning, Henry E., 131
Medieval prayer, 214
Merton, Thomas, 189
Metropolitan Philaret of Moscow, 203
Micklem, C, 12
Milner-White, Eric, 8, 150, 205
Morgan, Herbert, 158
Mother Teresa, 91, 120, 157, 162, 192
Mothers' Union Service Book, 165
Mozarabic Sacramentary, 46, 236
Muhammed, 115
Muslim prayer, 71

N
New Every Morning, 185
Newman, John Henry, 14, 58, 97, 217
Nicholas, W. Rhys, 105
Niebuhr, Reinhold, 177
Nitobe, Inazo, 45
Nouwen, Henri, 125, 191
Numbers 6:24-26, 234

O
Origen, 16, 127

P
Papyrus (probably 2nd-4th century), 47
Paton, Alan, 59, 111, 160, 201
Patrick, St, 238
Pite, A. G., 79

R
Rahulabhdra, 73
Rauschenbusch, Walter, 64
Ravensbruch, 84
Rees, Alan, 3, 78, 83, 88, 90, 95, 98, 106, 119, 133, 186, 200, 206, 210, 213, 215, 223
Reform Synagogues of Great Britain, 96
Richard of Chichester, St, 66
Richards, H. J., 183
Ridding, George, 122
Rosetti, Christina, 130
Runcie, Robert, 184
Russian, 178
Russian Orthodox, 222

S
Sergieff, John, 48
Shaw, Martin, 6, 149, 161
Sheppard, Dick, 153
Simeon the Theodidact, 5
Sioux, 197
Starck, Johann, 126
Swedish Liturgy, 172

T
Tagore, Rabindranath, 41
Taylor, Jeremy, 109, 141, 188, 239
Teresa of Avila, St, 76, 116
Thomas, T. Glyn, 105
Thomas Aquinas, St, 20, 44, 123
Toc H, 154
Traditional, 34, 87
Traditional Irish, 23
Traditional Scottish, 68

V
Vaughan, Charles John, 171

W
Weimarischer Gesangbuch, 227
Wesley, John, 121
Westcott, Brook Foss, 50, 103
Wilson, Thomas, 86
World Council of Churches, 80

Acknowledgements

The prayers listed below are in copyright. The addresses of copyright holders are given at the end of this section. The publishers wish to thank all those who have given their permission to reproduce copyright material in this publication.

8 © The Friends of York Minster
12 © SCM Press (*Contemporary Prayers* edited by Caryl Micklem, 1993)
15 Copyright Control
22 © Darton Longman & Todd Ltd (*Catholic Prayer Book*, 1970)
36 © USPG (*Prayer is my Life* by Margaret Dewey, 1966)
45 Copyright Control
56 © Wolfe Publishing Ltd
59 © Harper San Francisco (*Instrument of Thy Peace* by Alan Paton)
69 © Hodder Headline PLC (*God of our Fathers* edited by Frank Colquhoun)
74 © Hodder Headline PLC (*The Treasury of the Holy Spirit* edited by Tony Castle)
79 Copyright Control
80 © World Council of Churches
89 © SCM Press (*A Barclay Prayer Book* by William Barclay)
91 © Missionaries of Charity
96 © Reform Synagogues of Great Britain (*Form of Prayers for Jewish Worship, Vol III, Days of Awe Prayerbook*, 1977)
105 © Hodder Headline PLC (*God of our Fathers* edited by Frank Colquhoun)
111 © Harper San Francisco (*Instrument of Thy Peace* by Alan Paton)
120 © Missionaries of Charity
125 © Rev Henri Nouwen
150 © The Friends of York Minster
154 © Toc H
155 © Cardinal Basil Hume
157 © Missionaries of Charity
158 © Hodder Headline PLC (*God of our Fathers* edited by Frank Colquhoun)
159 © Christian Renewal Centre
160 © Harper San Francisco (*Instrument of Thy Peace* by Alan Paton)
162 © Missionaries of Charity
163 Copyright Control
164 Copyright Control
165 © The Mothers' Union
166 © Mambo Press
175 © Hodder Headline PLC (*The Pain that Heals* by Martin Israel)
177 Copyright Control
184 © Lord Runcie
185 © British Broadcasting Corporation
189 Burns & Oates Ltd (*Elected Silence* by Thomas Merton)
191 © Rev Henri Nouwen
192 © Missionaries of Charity
195 Copyright Control
196 © SCM Press (*A Kind of Praying* by Rex Chapman, 1970)
201 © Harper San Francisco (*Instrument of Thy Peace* by Alan Paton)
205 © The Friends of York Minster
220 Copyright Control
225 © SCM Press (*Letters and Papers from Prison* by Dietrich Bonhoeffer, Enlarged Edition, 1971)

The following prayers from *The Fount Book of Prayer* edited by Robert Van de Weyer are © HarperCollins Publishers Ltd: 5, 16, 43, 44, 46, 47, 48, 61, 73, 76, 92, 115, 123, 127, 135, 197

The following prayers are all © Kevin Mayhew Ltd: 2, 3, 6, 7, 10, 13, 14, 23, 29, 30, 38, 40, 42, 51, 53, 57, 58, 60, 63, 64, 65, 70, 77, 78, 82, 83, 85, 87, 88, 90, 93, 94, 95, 98, 102, 103, 106, 119, 122, 129, 132, 133, 134, 138, 139, 140, 142, 145, 146, 147, 149, 151, 152, 161, 176, 178, 179, 180, 182, 183, 186, 194, 198, 200, 206, 208, 210, 213, 214, 215, 223, 229, 230, 231

British Broadcasting Corporation, White City, 201 Wood Lane, London W12 7TS.
Burns & Oates Ltd, Wellwood, North Farm Road, Tunbridge Wells, Kent TN2 3DR.
Christian Renewal Centre, Shore Road, Rostrevor, Newry, Co. Down BT34 3ET, Northern Ireland.
Darton Longman & Todd Ltd, 1 Spencer Court, 140-142 Wandsworth High Street, London SW18 4JJ.
The Friends of York Minster, Church House, Ogleforth, York YO1 2JN.
Harper San Francisco, 1160 Battery Street, San Francisco, CA 94111, USA.
HarperCollins Publishers Ltd, 77-85 Fulham Palace Road, Hammersmith, London W6 8JB.
Hodder Headline PLC, 338 Euston Road, London NW1 3BH.
Mambo Press, Senga Road, PO Box 779, Gweru, Zimbabwe.
Missionaries of Charity, 54a Lower Circular Road, Calcutta 700016, India.
The Mothers' Union, The Mary Sumner House, 24 Tufton Street, London SW1P 3RB.
Reform Synagogues of Great Britain, The Sternberg Centre for Judaism, 80 East End Road, Finchley, London N3 2SY.
SCM Press Ltd, 26-30 Tottenham Road, London N1 4BZ.
Toc H, 1 Forest Close, Wendover, Aylesbury, Buckinghamshire, HP22 6BT.
The United Society for the Propagation of the Gospel (USPG), Partnership House, 157 Waterloo Road, London SE1 8XA.
Wolfe Publishing Ltd, Brooke House, 2-16 Torrington Place, London WC1E 7LT.
World Council of Churches, 150 Route de Ferney, PO Box 2100, 1211 Geneva 2, Switzerland.

Every effort has been made to trace the owners of copyright material and we hope that no copyright has been infringed. Pardon is sought and apology made if the contrary be the case, and a correction will be made in any reprint of this book.